T0193210

SHIFT

Indigenous Principles for Corporate Change

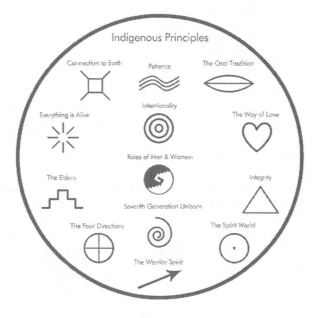

Indigenous Principles

Connection to Earth · Patience · The Oral Tradition · Everything is Alive · Intentionality · The Way of Love · Roles of Men & Women · The Elders · Integrity · Seventh Generation Unborn · The Four Directions · The Spirit World · The Warrior Spirit

GLENN GEFFCKEN

OPEN BOOK
EDITIONS
A Berrett–Koehler Partner

SHIFT
INDIGENOUS PRINCIPLES FOR CORPORATE CHANGE

iUniverse books may be ordered through booksellers or by contacting:

iUniverse
1663 Liberty Drive
Bloomington, IN 47403
www.iuniverse.com
1-800-Authors (1-800-288-4677)

Book cover art by Whoosh Kaallii
Book cover design by Michael G. Rey

ISBN: 978-1-4917-2661-7 (sc)
ISBN: 978-1-4917-2662-4 (e)

Library of Congress Control Number: 2014903422

Printed in the United States of America.

iUniverse rev. date: 03/20/2014

In loving memory of Pauline Bedonie,
from whom I have learned so much
about the traditional ways of being.

And in loving memory of Eas Yellowhair,
for you gave us hope that there are those
of the younger generation willing
and ready to carry the old ways forward.

Ten percent of proceeds from the sale
of this book arc being donated to nonprofits
engaged in assisting and helping indigenous elders.

Contents

Part III: Integration

Acknowledgments

I cannot begin to acknowledge and thank all those who have contributed to this work in so many ways, as this book is the result of a lifelong journey of exploration into human consciousness, cultural values, worldviews, philosophies, and daily practices for living. Such a journey can only happen through the synchronous involvement of hundreds of individuals and catalyzing events. Not only is deep gratitude and thanks owed to those who have provided teachings, help in times of need, love, and support, but I also owe a debt of gratitude to those who have brought hardship and discomfort to my life, as they have contributed to my growing strength and deepening understandings.

First and foremost, I would like to thank my beautiful wife, Maria, as she has been a steadfast source of support and encouragement. There were times when I felt it was a little crazy to be spending so much time writing when it would seem as though my priorities should have been elsewhere. In these times, Maria helped me to stay focused on the vision and importance of this work. She has provided guidance and invaluable input all along the way and has also provided the first round of copyediting, reading each chapter after I wrote it and helping me to polish as I went.

I would like to thank my adopted Navajo family, the Bedonie family of the Naakaii Dine'é clan (Mexican Bear clan). To my brother Daniel, as we have walked together for many years through many trials, teachings, travels, and amazing ceremonies together, your wisdoms run deep, and I have learned so much from you. To my late sister Pauline, thank you for your gentle loving ways, teachings from the old ones, and respect for the old ways. I never met your parents, but I'm sure I would have loved them. Thank you to Rolando for always making us laugh and being who you are.

Thank you, Geoff Fennel, for all your support, teachings, and love throughout the years. You've left an indelible mark in my life in so many ways. Thank you, Gen Wood, for all your prayers and for the huge support and help you provided in times of my greatest need. Thank you, Aldred Wood, your words are few, but so important. I learn from your humility all the time, and the work you've done for me in the tepee is beyond my ability to communicate in words.

Thank you, Walt Jacquez. We haven't exchanged too many words over the years, and the few words we did exchange were mostly in humorous moments, but please know that you have taught me a great deal through your example. I can see now what I couldn't have known back in 1997 when we first met—that the spirit of the old ways lives strong in you. I also remember you introducing me to people as a writer and me correcting you, saying that I wasn't. I think you saw in me what was to become. Thank you.

Thank you to the Rey family: Michael, Roberta, Analia, and Elaina. You gave me hope and a new vision for the life I have since grown into. Thank you, Michael Rey, for all the professional help you've provided, including the cover design for this book, in addition to and most importantly, for being you. Thank you, Lanny Kaufer, for your wisdom and compassion. Thank you, Joe DeVere, for who you are—and Rosanna too. Thank you, Sandy Jacquez, I've learned a great deal from you. Thank you to Sean Buck, Kenny Redhorse, Andrew Alvarez, Mark and Kathleen Chambers, Casey Marie Smith, Diane Black, Susan Rawcliffe, Mat Williams, and Henry Paul. Thank you, John Castillo. Thank you, Manly Littlebrave, for all your wisdom and love. Thank you, Terry Nations, for your own special brand of hillbilly humor and for all your wisdoms. Thank you, Terry Shin, for your stories and sensitivities. Thank you, Tommy Rosen, for being a catalyst for change.

Thank you, Samantha, Shana, and Kanyon. Through your sensitivity, you've continually challenged me to be more fully present with all that is and all that I am feeling.

Thank you, Father, for being one of my greatest cheerleaders and for your ongoing support for my writing. Thank you brother Ron, your support has been meaningful in ways you'll never know.

Thank you, Becky Herdt, for all that you do; you are a true blessing and gift to the world. Thank you, Alder and Isabel for believing in this work and supporting us in our efforts. Thank you, Keresey Proctor and Andy Crespo, for understanding and embracing the vision of the indigenous ways and translating that so elegantly to video. Thank you, Keith Vallely, Meridith Elliot Powell, Justin Belleme, and the team at JB Media. Thank you to my editor, Jennifer Flynn, for the great collaboration and for understanding my vision. Thank you, Steve Collins, for modeling for the cover art and for your kindness. Thank you, Jonathan Pulsifer and Howard Furst.

To the spirit realm, thank you to all the ancestors who have walked with me, helped and guided me when I've asked, and spoken through me and who help me gradually, lovingly, and consistently to discover my purpose and to live that life.

Introduction

> Today, what is important for us is to realize that the old sacred
> ways are correct, and that if we do not follow them, we will be lost
> and without a guide.
>
> —Thomas Yellowtail, Crow

Without intending to, in the summer of 1997, I embarked on a parallel
course in life, one foot firmly planted in the corporate world and the
other in the world of North American Native religious ceremonies and
culture. While it took some time to realize how these two seemingly
disparate tracks in life could actually have congruency or correlation,
what I indeed discovered was that this parallel held a key to great
understanding for both.

This book is about drawing corollaries and distinctions, but
primarily about drawing wisdoms from the teaching of indigenous
culture and their implications for significant transformation of core
behaviors, attitudes, beliefs, values, and ethics, which taken as a whole
represent a paradigm shift on an order of magnitude rarely seen in the
business world.

Paradigm shift has long since been established as a buzz phrase
and the golden goose for any executive who can actually accomplish it
successfully. There have been a significant number of books written on
the topic, and so many authors, consultants, and executives talk about
it in terms of how to accomplish it and how to make the changes stick.
Many of the best books and teachings by business thought leaders
on the topic of culture and paradigm shift are right on the money in

terms of how organizations need to behave, yet actually effecting the change in a dramatic and lasting way is what is most difficult. How do we motivate a certain set of behaviors in a large organization, or even small- to medium-sized organizations? How do we engender a particular kind of vibration or feeling within an organization that leads to a desired outcome? Or stated more simply: How do we create a thriving organizational culture?

As I have discovered, there is a very definite way to accomplish this. The how comes directly from the teachings of cultures that those in the business world may tend to think of as oversimplistic, primitive, superstitious, and ritualistic, which may explain why the business world has overlooked the applicability of indigenous teachings to the complex, fast-moving, and rapidly changing world of business and commerce.

This book, and the process provided herein, offers a near foolproof methodology, which if practiced consistently, earnestly, and authentically will bring about the very cultural paradigm shift we need. While the origin of this system may seem unorthodox and unusual, it is drawn from a people who have lived in harmony with nature, and for the most part each other, for eons of time. Encoded within the DNA of their cultural paradigm is the framework for the perpetuation and continual enhancement of their culture, which has stood the test of time. Their principles, as offered in this book, are directly applicable to the world of business; and through them, we can powerfully transform our business and organizational culture in ways that will remedy the issues of balance with nature, with humanity, and with employees and constituents, and drive a feeling within our organizations that will empower people to higher levels of performance, creativity, and innovation.

The Need for Change

What we are growing in awareness of is that constant change is the only constant and that business needs to shift its way of doing things; its culture; its ethics; the very paradigm for how we make things, ship them, and sell them; the services provided; and how we structure our businesses. With the immediacy of the Internet, the shift from mass marketing to niche marketing, virtually unlimited buying choices, and rapidly advancing technology, the challenge of growing a business requires continuous evolution.

Even our social culture is changing, and not always for the better. Therefore, the way we communicate our brand message and reach our audience must continually shift so that we may continue to connect with our audience in a meaningful way. Organizational cultural change requires that our brand itself must evolve in order to stay fresh and compelling in the marketplace. However, the paramount need for change is related more to our ethical framework for doing business and the results it brings.

For example, we are presently consuming natural resources for the perpetuation of our present culture at rates far faster than nature can replenish them. We are upsetting the delicate balance of our ecosystems to such an extent that we are experiencing a mass extinction of plant and animal species at rates far faster than any of the prior mass extinctions that have been so thoroughly studied and documented.[1] Nearly every credible scholar in the field of ecology agrees that nearly all our living ecosystems are in decline and that all factors point to the mass scale of human consumption as the catalyzing force in this decline.

Therefore, it makes little sense for us to perpetuate our culture and ways of doing things without giving deep consideration to the fact that we could very well be consuming ourselves out of existence; that to enjoy our present level of prosperity and physical comfort, we are making it impossible for future generations to survive in similar comfort—or to survive at all.

Slavery in the modern world is another example of the urgent need for change, as it is a little-known fact that there is more slavery in the world today (twenty-seven million) than when President Abraham Lincoln signed the Emancipation Proclamation Act in 1862.[2] Slavery today looks very different than it did in the pre-Civil War era, when slave owners openly and proudly displayed their use of slavery to produce products, grow food, raise animals, clean their homes, and take care of their children. Today slaves are called factory workers or nannies or prostitutes for hire; when people are not free to leave their employment and seek a better life, are forced to work long hours physically locked in a building, are beaten and intimidated when taking restroom breaks, and make below subsistence wages, they are tantamount to slaves. There are many millions of people in places like Ghana, Nepal, and India suffering the most brutal form of slavery, working seventeen hours per day without pay, without freedom, interacting with toxic chemicals and dying young related to the work they do.[3]

The causes of slavery in the modern world are many. In some cases, it is due to pure selfishness, insensitivity, and cruelty on the level of the individuals who enslave or who utilize the services of slaves. On another level, it exists because large organizations and countries turn a blind eye because there is a significant financial advantage to do so. In some cases, slavery is condoned or ignored for political reasons; in other instances, it is because of businesses remaining so disconnected from their supply chains as to be unaware of the oppressive practices of their suppliers.

Slavery, along with wide-scale environmental degradation, is the proverbial canary in the coal mine, telling us that something is fundamentally wrong with our collective organizational culture, the construct of how we do business.

There is also a growing dissatisfaction among modern businesspeople with the constant hectic nature of their work. Endless streams of e-mails, myriad projects, lengthy meetings, and too many competing objectives taxing our emotional and mental energy have given way to a trend of people striving and struggling to find work/life balance. Many executives I have spoken with about the concept of work/life balance believe that it isn't possible to achieve; they have fatalistically accepted that they will *always* be struggling to keep up with the pace of work while trying in some way to find a semblance of balance with home and family.

There is also a growing dissatisfaction with the meaningfulness of our work; many in business feel a lack of connection with the companies with whom they work and a lack of an emotional or visceral alignment with their goals and objectives. A recent Gallup survey conducted over thirteen years shows a consistent level of employee disengagement of roughly 70 percent.[4] While some might argue that that number seems much too high and that survey methodology has a lot to do with how people answer questions related to their emotional connection to their company, it is safe to say, based on the research, that this is a huge problem facing corporate leadership and significantly contributes to lackluster performance on an organizational level.

Our Corporate Value System

For some, it is easier to believe that our social, environmental, and cultural shortcomings are related to a certain few "bad apples," or that we are making progress and need to maintain our optimism, or that technological advancements will solve our problems, or that we are on the verge of great positive change. All these notions may, in fact, be true, but the anticipated technological, social, and corporate culture shifts will not manifest themselves without an honest acceptance of our current situation and a willingness to effect change on a fundamental level—the level of the principles and values that make up our cultural fabric.

Technology, for example, works at the hands of those who wield it; therefore, the application of technology has more to do with our core intentions and values than the technology itself. Therefore, we must change ourselves, our cultural fabric including our values and principles, so that we may first know where and how to direct technological developments that will bring about the highest and best good for all. Then we must have the willingness to put those resulting advancements to use on a mass scale. Another example is how some people say that "guns kill people." But guns don't go off by themselves; rather they require people to wield them—either constructively or harmfully.

When companies make decisions with life-and-death consequences based largely on financial objectives and do so consistently, we can see that our corporate value system is upside down; that the business entities, the constructs created for the purpose of facilitating business and commerce, have become the master and the people the slaves. Our corporate and economic value system, as implied by outward results, illustrates that we have created a world that places business objectives before human objectives; environmental degradation, slavery, and the loss of purposeful work serve as three examples of the upside-down nature of our corporate value system.

I am not suggesting that everyone making decisions in a corporate environment has an intention of hurting people or the planet; rather, the construct of the corporation, whether it be an LLC, partnership, C corp, or S corp, is such that we give a sense of life to the business construct itself, independent of its people, and the construct is one in which the primary objective is typically to deliver profit in ever-increasing amounts. The construct could, therefore, be said to drive the culture, and the culture drives the actions of its people. Presently our collective construct is based on an ethic that values the business entity more greatly than the people who comprise the business entity.

The Purpose of Business

I've never personally seen scary-looking men in black suits coming out of the offices of executives who are engaged in making bad decisions, but I *have* heard the voice of the construct, the ever-persistent whisper in our ear that seemingly comes from some unknowable yet tangible higher power and says, "Profit is good," "Profit is everything," "Cutting costs is always good," and "After all, we're not a charity." There are plenty more presumed axioms that speak to us so softly and subtly, yet with the force of a thousand voices.

The question at hand is, is not the purpose of business to serve us, *humanity*, to provide for an enjoyable way of life, to provide for our families, to enable us to pursue other enjoyable activities outside of our work, such as family, social activities, religion, spirituality, leisure, art, and perpetual learning? Is business not simply a vehicle for our daily living, a tool for life?

When we place business and its construct at the foremost level of importance, have we not turned our world upside down; have we not made ourselves the servants of the tools of our survival, rather than the tools of our survival being the servants of those who wield them? A carpenter does not go to work to serve his hammer and saw. The hammer and saw serve the carpenter, and in this way, the construct of business ought to be such that it serves the greater good.

The Voice of the Ancestors

When we allow ourselves to be driven by the voice of a construct that demands profits above all else, we are taking our focus off the most important things that can lead to true prosperity and a kind of success that brings fulfillment and meaning. In this way, we are allowing the voice of the construct to drown out another voice, a voice that for many of us is almost too quiet to hear, a voice that yearns to be heard, to be given attention, and cultivated. This is the voice that the indigenous principles speak to, the voice of values, meaning, and purpose, or as some would refer to it, the voice of the ancestors.

As I have discovered, by practicing the indigenous principles, one can give strength to the quiet voice within, the voice that deeply resonates with the timeless ancient wisdoms of the elders, the whisper of nature, the dormant passions, and the need to transcend the dominant corporate culture that continually says, "More profit."

The Purpose of Change

An upside-down world cannot logically continue to exist in perpetuity without great change brought on willfully and intentionally, or otherwise catalyzed by catastrophic shifts in external conditions that render the status quo inoperable. We have seen many industries become obsolete over time as technological advances change the playing field, and there have been huge organizations that have fallen by the wayside due to their inability to change with the times. Spending eleven years working for a big-city newspaper at a time when the newspaper industry was undergoing dramatic shifts was a painful experience; I watched so many well-meaning individuals with an incredible awareness of the need to change and yet possessing very little sense of how to do it.

The need for change is great, but not change for change's sake. We need the kind of change that moves our society toward the ideal of healthy balance—balance with people, planet, and profit, otherwise known as the three Ps, or the triple bottom line. We need to expand our business objectives to incorporate human, social, and environmental benefits, along with profitability, not greater than or less than, but equal to in importance.

The Nature of Change

A recent advancement addressing the need for positive change is the movement of many state legislatures to adopt benefit corporations as a legal business structure. At the time of this writing, nineteen states— Arizona, Arkansas, California, Colorado, Hawaii, Illinois, Louisiana, Maryland, Massachusetts, Nevada, New Jersey, New York, Oregon, Pennsylvania, South Carolina, Vermont, Virginia, Washington DC, and most recently Delaware—have adopted such legislation, in which businesses can establish themselves as benefit corporations, a legal structure that requires its directors to serve the combined objectives of purpose, accountability, and transparency, in addition to profitability.

In *The Ecology of Commerce*, Paul Hawken powerfully suggests a new ethical model most succinctly. "Just as every act in an industrial society leads to environmental degradation, regardless of intention, we must design a system where the opposite is true, where doing good is like falling off a log, where the natural, everyday acts of work and life accumulate into a better world as a matter of course, not a matter of conscious altruism."[5] Future generations require that we transform our business culture and move it in the direction of ideals that bring about fairness, respect, and balance with nature.

The landmark book *Firms of Endearment*, by authors Sisodia, Wolfe, and Sheth, powerfully illustrates how businesses fundamentally driven by humanistic values have significantly outperformed the S&P 500 by a factor of more than eight to one.[6]

Internationally respected consultant, author, and professor Gary Hamil has eloquently illustrated how the concept of management was created in the late nineteenth and early twentieth centuries for the purpose of getting employees to work in a mechanized environment consistently and efficiently, "but in so doing it squanders prodigious quantities of human imagination and initiative."[7] Hamil's prescription for change can be summarized as, "The only way to build a company that's fit for the future is to build one that's fit for human beings as well."[8]

There are numerous thought leaders who have identified the need for humanizing change, and many of them, like Hawken, Sisodia, Wolf, Sheth, and Hamil mentioned above, are clearly on the right track.

The nature of change required to restore us to balance and harmony requires that we look beyond the prevailing corporate mantra of profit first, that we open our minds to new ways of doing things, and that we right-side-up our priorities related to a corporate construct that serves humanity and is in balance with our ecosystem.

Defining *Indigenous*

Throughout this book I will be referring to the people and culture from which I have learned these wisdoms as indigenous people and indigenous culture. It is important to address the limitation of language when it comes to truly identifying the culture and principles that we are speaking of. We can say *Native American*, which typically refers only to North American Native people. We can say *Indian*, yet that term is so vague as it evolved from a misperception on the part of Christopher Columbus that he had arrived in India from the east, not a whole other continent less than halfway around the world. We can use the term *indigenous*, yet the concept of indigenous is the most vague of all, as all people are essentially indigenous to some place on Earth.

We can also say *tribal*, which may be the most accurate, yet tribal does not have to imply an Earth-based or ancient culture. Indeed, author Seth Godin has drawn a powerful set of behaviors from tribal culture as applicable to the business world, which many organizations are utilizing to transform their behaviors.[9]

So, what does *indigenous* really mean? I will apologize in advance to the reader for any potential lack of clarity in these definitions, and yet I will say at the outset that while I tend toward the use of *indigenous*, I am generally referring to people from cultures that are rooted in a strong connection to Mother Earth, that are tribal in nature, and that have some degree of connection to the traditions of their ancestors that stretches back for more than a thousand years.

Indigenous People Are Alike

While the majority of my training in indigenous culture is specific to North America, and more specifically to the culture of the Navajo or Dinéh people, I am also generally referring to indigenous people from all across the world, as there are many fundamental principles related to their cultures that are startlingly similar from one end of the globe to another.

As an example of this similarity, the International Council of Thirteen Indigenous Grandmothers serves as a powerful guidepost to both the implications and universal nature of indigenous wisdom. They are thirteen elder grandmothers, representing Alaska, North America, South America, Central America, Africa, and Asia. Since 2004, these grandmothers have been convening annually, each time hosted by a different grandmother, traveling around the world and growing closer to one another in their unified purpose of representing "a global alliance of prayer, education and healing for our Mother Earth, all Her inhabitants, all the children, and for the next seven generations to come." They are deeply concerned about the destruction of our environment and "indigenous ways of life," as their mission statement declares and goes on to say, "We believe the teachings of our ancestors will light our way through an uncertain future."[10]

The profound implication of their alliance is to understand that indigenous people from around the globe are far more similar than different. While their formalities and rituals may vary, their core values are essentially the same. They are all deeply rooted in a connection to Earth. They regularly engage in ceremonies of renewal. They utilize natural elements (plants, roots, and herbs) as offerings and to burn for cleansing. They believe very deeply in a connection to a spirit world. Their lineage is very important to them. They believe that their old traditions are important to their survival, and principally they believe that our modern world is in a state of sickness. These notions are universally held in common among indigenous people the world over.

Indigenous People Persevere

As mentioned previously, indigenous cultures are the only cultures to have lived successfully in perfect harmony with nature for thousands of years, and not just some indigenous cultures, but all of them. For all of our technology and intelligence, mechanization, creature comforts, modern health care, understanding of science, education, and complex systems of government, business, and economics, we do not know how to live in harmony with our natural world. We seek to overpower nature, and the more we do so, the more we upset the balance of our ecosystem.

Presently there are few places left on Earth in which there are indigenous people living completely untouched by modern society. There are a few small pockets living in primitive style, while the majority of indigenous cultures have been contaminated to a great extent by modern culture. In North America, the genetic susceptibility of Native Americans to alcoholism and diabetes and how these diseases ravage their families and communities are widely known. Indigenous people the world over struggle significantly to partially assimilate into modern society, just enough to survive, while still retaining their heritage, their languages, ceremonies, and values.

Then again, within these cultures is an incredible resiliency in spite of unbelievable racism, oppression, cultural contamination, even genocide; they still hold onto the essence of who they are and why they are here on God's given Mother Earth. It is from this resiliency and perseverance to their ceremonial traditions, teachings of the elders, and core values that myself and so many others have been able to benefit.

There is still enough left of their cultures to come to an understanding of what it truly means to be indigenous. Indeed, there is truly enough left to derive their underlying values and principles and to learn from them, reform our addictions, heal our relationships, and transform our working world to a world of success as defined more broadly as a balance of objectives, including having an enjoyable lifestyle, holding to high ethics, honoring our relationships (all of them), being truly fulfilled in what we do, and moving in the direction of balance with nature. All of these objectives taken as a whole and achieved will naturally and as a by-product of our efforts also deliver economic prosperity, as I have witnessed.

The Invitation

This exploration is about the how it is that we make a living, where the fulfillment we seek, the ethics we adhere to, the relationships we form and cultivate, and the lifestyle we live are *all* of high importance.

Creating a world that is sustainable is also of paramount importance, as we will cease to exist if we deteriorate our living systems, our biosphere, to such an extent that radically affects the ability of future generations to perpetuate themselves. In short, this exploration is based on the premise that *how we make a living is equally as important as doing so.*

I realize that the premise of this book may seem overly strong to some, as I'm suggesting that we need significant core change, that our business construct is upside down, that we have subrogated human values for corporate values, and that corporate values consist largely of an abstract need for ever-increasing profits. More importantly, I recognize and can appreciate how hard it is to break from a common understanding. The construct of the modern world speaks to us in a continuous flow of economic indicators, jobs reports, interest rates, credit ratings, market share, technological advancements, and on and on. It takes willingness and an open mind to break free from common thinking and to consider radically different perspectives.

The invitation I'm offering in this book is to break free and consider a different course. This does not mean that you cannot return to your previous thinking or retain your present ideological approach to business; rather, it means there is an opportunity to gain hugely from the wisdoms of the indigenous people, wisdoms that can cast a light of clarity on the pathway to core change, the kind of change that can restore us to balance and harmony.

Part I: Two Worlds Become One

A good heart and a good mind—those are what you need to be a chief.

—Louis Farmer, Onondaga

Chapter 1. One Fine Morn

> Growth is a painful process.
> —Wilma Mankiller, Cherokee

On one fine morning in the summer of 1997, after having spent some three years or so inching my way into the Native America powwow culture, I was invited to a Native American religious ceremony, and without knowing what I was getting myself into, the word *yes* flew right out of my mouth.

I was introduced to the world of powwows through my first wife, a woman of Lakota decent, who had been raised by an Italian family and discovered some elements of her heritage through majoring in Native American studies in college. It was through random invitations from friends that we found ourselves regularly attending powwows on the weekends.

While there are many non-Indians who feel a certain drive to learn from, be a part of, and gain acceptance by Native American people, I don't think I have ever been driven that way. Yet I recall my first two powwows distinctly for the radical difference in culture that I observed and found highly compelling. The starkest contrast I saw to the modern culture I grew up in was the complete and total integration of all ages into one collective social gathering and celebration. I observed children barely past the point of having taken their first steps dancing around in a circle alongside teenagers, adults, and elders well into their eighties, all together with one unified drum and song. I found it beautiful, and it felt like home.

At my second powwow, I watched a coming-out ceremony performed for a young boy who was coming out as a northern traditional powwow dancer. The ceremony was conducted by a man I assumed to be a father or uncle, who took him around the circle, stopping at each of the four directions, who leaned down to speak softly into his ear, appearing to convey some great teaching or wisdom. Then as the drumming and singing started, the boy danced around the circle alone, as the official coming-out as a young man and a dancer tasked with maintaining the traditions and respect for the old ways. Watching this young boy dancing in a large circle for all to see with such grace and dignity was moving.

I was very much taken by this simple rite of passage. I observed what seemed like a deep respect from everyone present for the importance of what was taking place; a hush fell over the arena, with focused attention and a seeming mutual understanding for the experience of a lifetime for a young boy discovering his path in life.

This cultural unity and identity is what attracted me to powwows and compelled me to seek more of it. I knew then of how so many non-Indians attach a certain romanticism to Native culture, possessing an image of a proud people riding swiftly on horseback with the wind flowing in their long hair, feathers draping gracefully from hair and clothing, made of buckskins and beads. Personally, the only Indians I have met like this lived in Southern California, had headshots and agents, and mostly worked as extras in the film business.

The Indians that I have known have been as varied as any other culture I've experienced, and yet most, but not all, have possessed some similarities that I have continued to find enjoyable and enriching, such as a sweet and playful sense of humor, a slow deliberative way of communicating, and an intuitive sense that land and respect for it are extremely important, that elders are people to be highly regarded, that *Little House on the Prairie* is really good television, and that family and lineage is how a person identifies one's self.

I made friends in the powwow circuit, some become close friends, and one in particular, a Comanche brother named John, phoned me on that one fine morning in the summer of 1997 to ask if I wanted to take part in an actual Native American religious ceremony. With drumming and singing and God knows what else, I had no idea what was in store for me. And what I did not yet know was that all that I thought I had learned about their culture, their ways and values, was only scratching the surface; that simple coming-out ceremonies or their sense of humor or even their pride in lineage could not begin to shed light on the depth of purpose and values that are so deeply engrained in their culture. I could never have imagined the journey I was about to embark on, what was in store for me, and the life that was to flow from dedicating much of my life to their spiritual ways and teachings.

So there I was, several days later, sitting in this ceremony, referred to in the casual sense as a house meeting—a meeting yes, conducted in a house yes, but really a ceremony with roots that stretch back for thousands of years as far as we can tell, with ancient songs, use of natural elements such as sage and cedar, a drum, a gourd rattle, tobacco, and lots and lots of prayer.

There was a man affectionately referred to as the sponsor, who provided the purpose for which we were gathered together to pray, who was suffering from a life-threatening disease. There was a roadman, who conducted the ceremony; and a fire man, who maintained a fire outside the house and continually brought coals in, from which cedar was burned for purification. There was a drummer; a water woman, which I didn't really understand at the time; and some thirty or so other people, all seated in a circle having come to pray for the sponsor and blessings in their own lives. Many were Native, but most were not.

We started right at sundown and continued all through the night until a couple hours past sunrise. We did not sleep or eat. We sat on the floor in a circle on folded blankets and struggled to keep focus on prayer and song, without conversation or distraction.

The experience for me was nothing short of completely miserable. My feeling driving home was that those people were crazy to want to go to such ceremonies, experience such sacrifice and physical discomfort, and then to go back again and again as they do. Yet the peace that came over me in the days following was indescribable. Somehow, and in rather short order, I developed the desire to get back into another ceremony. I called my good friend and started inquiring about the next ceremony.

What I thought of myself at the time of my first ceremony was that I was a very spiritual person, as I had always had an inclination in that direction, had studied many different philosophies, had practiced and learned about many different traditions, had read all kinds of self-help books, and had meditated, yet I had never really understood what prayer actually was until that first ceremony. Miserable as I was through long hours of focus, with my back, butt, and legs in pain, dehydrated, nauseous, and with a headache, something happened for me, something I could not quite define until a few years later, something profound and powerful; and yet it would be another ten to fifteen years before I came to fully understand what the road I had taken was and where it was leading.

Thus began my most amazing journey of self-discovery, transformation, and happiness.

Chapter 2. In Parallel

Dissimilar things were fitted together to make something beautiful and whole.

—Nippawanock, Arapahoe

In parallel to my journey in the world of Native American spirituality was a gradually advancing career in the business world. I was young in business at the time of my initiation into Native American culture, and outside of a desire to work in and around sustainability, I had no sense that a parallel purpose could potentially exist. As it took me many years to discover my purpose in Native spirituality, it took equally as long to discover its parallel to my working life.

Graduating from college in 1990 with a degree in criminal justice, I initially thought of continuing on to law school, and for many reasons, not the least of which was the glut of lawyers in the market at the time, I decided instead to launch a plastics recycling business. Four years into that project and out of capital, I jumped into investment sales, thinking that that would be exciting, but for me it was not. Then I bumbled around in various sales jobs before landing a position at a big-city newspaper.

I worked extremely hard at the paper, received several promotions in my first two years, and wound up producing their large-scale consumer festivals and trade shows for the next nine years. Having launched a start-up, sold investments and business-to-business products, understood contract law and finance, I came to the newspaper business with an inordinate amount of knowledge of how business works, yet lacked many of the critical social and people skills necessary to be effective on all levels.

It was shortly after joining the paper that I attended my first Native American ceremony, and so my journey at the paper, being hard and messy as it was, paralleled my development in the tepees, sweat lodges, and house meetings. It was gradual at first. I experienced small imperceptible changes in my way of relating to the world and my relations with people. Over time, my personality shifted, along with my values and ethics, and in the process I found that I had become really good at my work. Then I realized that the improvement in my work had more to do with the frequent trips I was taking to the Navajo reservation in Arizona and New Mexico, and time spent with the elders, teachers, ceremonies, and being immersed in the culture, than from my business experience itself.

This was a crazy realization, as I felt like I had my feet in two completely different worlds and that the two worlds were incongruent. I realized what I was discovering was that all that does not work about the business world is really what is incongruent with tribal cultures with a strong connection to Mother Earth, and all that works beautifully in the business world is actually very compatible.

With this realization, I continued to progress on both fronts, seeking career advancement and continuing with the ceremonies and teachings from my Native relations.

I was recruited in 2008 by a boutique event company in North Carolina, which was great timing as I was at a stage in life where I felt the need for some big changes. So I left my California ceremony community and moved across the country. I also left behind a long and difficult marriage and a job that I felt had become stagnant. I took on the role of selling sponsorships to green and sustainability-related events, doing business development, formulating strategy, and managing a sales team.

I had my Navajo brother Daniel come out from Arizona to live with me for a short time. We built a sweat lodge and held ceremonies. We spent a great deal of time together, which enabled my training in the Navajo traditions to deepen. I also traveled around the East and

Midwest attending more ceremonies and connected with ceremony communities in North Carolina.

Moving to North Carolina was a great transition and provided me the opportunity to ease into more substantial life changes that were to come shortly after my relocation. In the three years with the boutique event company, I continued advancing my knowledge of Native culture and spirituality, and also grew immensely in business savvy. Yet again, I have to credit the work I was doing with indigenous culture and spirituality for the ways in which I advanced in capabilities related to my work.

In the summer of 2011, it became evident that it was time for me to fulfill more of my purpose and self-expression in the working world by branching out on my own and serving more than just one company. So I launched a consulting company and began the work of even more deeply discovering my true gifts to the world in relation to the work that I do.

This process of career self-discovery could never have occurred if I weren't in parallel, deeply advancing my understanding of my purpose related to my indigenous practices. By this stage in my life, the two courses and their inextricably linked nature had become self-evident.

Chapter 3. At Its Core

To be able to greet the sun with the sounds from all of Nature
is a great blessing, and it helps us to remember Who is the real
provider of all of our benefits.

—Thomas Yellowtail, Crow

The parallel I experienced in my walk with indigenous people and my
work in the business world can be described in relation to the core
purpose for our work in general. For example, how many of us would
continue in our present line of work if we just came into a large sum of
money? Most, I think, would promptly quit, or at least radically change
the nature of their work. We try to work at things that we generally
like. Some are lucky enough to work at things they truly love and are
passionate about, but more commonly, we work to make a living.

While ego gratification can serve as a powerful motivator guiding
us in our work, for some it is the accumulation of power and control
that drives them. Yet on a basic level, we are dealing with livelihood,
the method of our physical survival in life.

This purpose of basic survival is not incongruent with Earth-based
cultures; they just perceive a different paradigm around how to go about
accomplishing livelihood, and it is precisely this paradigm that is the
focus of this book, along with the underlying intention and intrinsic
core values that drive their way of being.

Simplistic as it may sound, it is important to make the distinction
that what we do at a core starts with the motivation of generating a
livelihood. So too with the values reflected in tribal-based cultures; they

are also about living, livelihood, and perpetuation. What we all hope for is a kind of life and work that supports our happiness and good health emotionally and physically, feels at least somewhat meaningful to us, and brings about prosperity and abundance.

I would ask the reader to consider this exploration to be a process. As we are dealing with core cultural differences, and as culture serves as a framework of beliefs and behaviors that bind us through commonality, contrasting cultures and understanding the value in their differences requires us to be willing to think differently. Even if only for a moment, we must imagine, what if the world were like this or that; or what if the axioms that we assume are valid are only so because we believe them to be; or what if a radically different way of life could actually be enjoyable, or at least no worse than the one we have; and so on.

F. Scott Fitzgerald once wrote, "The test of a first-rate intelligence is the ability to hold two opposed ideas in mind at the same time, and still retain the ability to function."[1] So I would ask the reader to follow along, enjoy the ride, and seek to channel a little bit of Fitzgerald in the process.

Beyond the value of grasping a radically different cultural perspective and learning from those differences, there is also the possibility of transforming the very paradigm, the model for our active engagement in the world, which can bring about success, fulfillment, and happiness on a level never before imagined.

I believe you can.

Chapter 4. Indigenous Principles

Search for the truth. Indian values teach the holistic approach to the use of technology for mankind's good.

—Al Qoyawayma, Hopi

Five years or so into my immersion into Native American spirituality, having taken many trips out to Native reservations, participated in dozens of ceremonies, and been adopted into a Navajo family, I found that I was changing on the inside in a subtle, almost imperceptible way. I found that I was becoming calmer, more patient, and wiser in my interactions with people. I still had a long way to go at the time, yet the changes were becoming manifest.

A few years after this point, it started to become more clear that the very principles that underlie indigenous culture were permeating into my thinking and way of being, that I was finding a direct applicability of these principles to the business world, and that they were empowering me to a less chaotic and more effective, fulfilling, and successful business career.

Beginning with the most basic of all indigenous principles, one that spans cultures from one end of the globe to the other—that we are all connected in a fundamental way to Earth—we could, in fact, stop right here and explore this one concept and its implications for our life, and find the topic to be vast. Yet there are many deeply profound and powerful principles shared universally within the realm of indigenous cultures, each of which provides far-reaching implications for a new paradigm of how to live our lives, be with our families and our communities, and conduct business.

For this exploration, I have selected thirteen indigenous principles (twelve in section II, and one in section III) to examine and digest, and have attempted to maintain a largely secular approach to indigenous culture so as to allow these principles to be palatable to the largest possible audience.

In my own spiritual journey, I have found far more in common among the great religions of the world than different, or perhaps it is that those tenets of religion that I personally find most appealing are those that tend to be in common with so many other philosophies—for example, the concept of there being one God, that we should all try and be kind, loving, and compassionate toward our fellow human beings, that we should strive toward charity and humility, and so on. I'm not so concerned with the differences in rituals, the songs sung, whether people pray on their knees on the ground or in pews or tepees; rather, I find it fascinating how different religions utilize different stories and language to convey essentially the same thing.

This is an important point to consider given that there is so much similarity among indigenous religions from one end of the globe to the other. Many would be surprised to find a great deal of similarity between indigenous religion and the predominant religions of the world such as Buddhism, Christianity, Judaism, and Islam, if we solely looked at religion with a lens that magnifies the meditative and altruistic components.

I have taken a mostly secular approach so as not to get caught up in splitting hairs over deeply held beliefs related to prayer, meditation, and a person's individual relationship with his or her higher power. For this reason, I have specifically organized and presented this book with the intention of providing universal principles that can be employed by everyone, regardless of their sectarian leanings or practices, even agnostics or atheists.

While there is a particular order in which the principles are presented, it is important to understand that this is a nonlinear process. Most people are already practicing some, if not many, of these principles. A few people practice all of them in a business dynamic to some extent. *All* of us can benefit from exploring them as a system and delving more deeply into them. Yet our pathway to exploration of indigenous principles will be different for every individual, as we all begin from our own unique perspective on values and culture. As we progress through the following chapters, you will see many references between the chapters, connecting and relating the principles. You may even feel like venturing back to reread prior chapters after having reached a certain level of understanding, or even jumping forward. This is to be expected and is encouraged so long as it is understood that the body of thirteen indigenous principles explored herein represent a complete system for catalyzing cultural change.

At this point it would be good to point out the irony of this exploration, in that I'm positing that the greatest business leaders of our time have some very important lessons to learn from these seemingly simple people, these "poor" Indians, that our indigenous people can somehow teach us how to do business better, while indigenous people struggle to barely survive in the modern world. Yes, it is an irony indeed, and yet it is true.

While most indigenous people who have been raised in a somewhat traditional environment struggle to function within the framework of our modern society, they hold the keys to positive transformation of our business dynamic. It is actually through their disorientation with our modern world that the teachings can flow. If they just merely adapted and blended in, we would never have an opportunity to explore how they are different from those of us rooted in the modern world, and we would never be inclined to distinguish and discern the sociological incompatibilities.

The reason they struggle so much to adapt is because the modern world is an alien world to the traditional indigenous person, and it is alien to indigenous people because it is upside down to them, which is precisely the point of this book. Adopting indigenous principles does not require that we cast aside our technology and creature comforts, don the leather and fringe, and ride a horse bareback into the sunset. It may, however, require that we make numerous lifestyle changes, as Al Qoyawayma stated in the quote at the beginning of this chapter that "Indian values teach the holistic approach to the use of technology for mankind's good."[1]

Indigenous principles and culture teach us how to realign our value systems toward balance and harmony with each other—between companies, communities, and countries—and with nature. They teach us to right-side-up our imperatives and to empower the carpenter to master the hammer and saw as his or her servants and tools for survival and perpetuation. Indigenous wisdoms give us the keys to shared prosperity and abundance, lives and work filled with meaning and purpose, and respect for all living things.

There is also an opportunity for both cultures to learn from one another, for our modern world to learn how to be in more balance with people and Earth, and for our indigenous people to learn more about adapting to our modern world without sacrificing all that is meaningful and important to their way of being.

In light of this realization, let us begin our exploration of indigenous principles.

Part II: The Principles Explored

Times change but principles do not. Times change but lands do not. Times change but our culture and our language remain the same. And that's what you have to keep intact. It's not what you wear—it's what's in your heart.

—Oren Lyons, Onondaga

Chapter 5. Connection to Earth

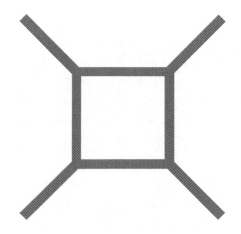

The old Lakota was wise. He knew that man's heart away from nature becomes hard; he knew the lack of respect for growing, living things soon led to a lack of respect for humans too. So he kept his youth close to its softening influence.

—Luther Standing Bear, Oglala Sioux

In this exploration of indigenous culture and principles, starting with their connection to Earth is an important launch point for understanding why indigenous people from one end of the globe to the other share so much philosophy in common. While on the surface level we have discussed how imperative it is to move ourselves in the direction of an economic system and culture that preserves and conserves natural resources, rather than consumes resources faster than they can be replenished, we have discussed this on a level of commonsense utilitarianism. Yet indigenous people do not walk in harmony with nature because it is the right thing to do or because it makes sense; they walk in harmony because it is the only relationship they know with nature.

Luther Standing Bear's quote touches on this, as one can only *touch* on this concept when attempting to describe how and why indigenous people are connected to Earth; that time spent with nature has a "softening influence." Again, there is much room for contrast to modern culture in that many people of our modern culture have the idea that time spent with nature looks like rolling into a campground in a massive RV and piling out with bicycles, mopeds, and coolers packed with beer and soda, and then comes the boom box.

To the indigenous perspective, this approach to nature is foolhardy, or at a minimum, misses the point. There is an important reason why their ceremonies involve rigorous personal sacrifice having to do with the natural elements. There is typically some amount of fasting involved, sitting on the ground for long periods of time, withstanding extremes of heat and cold, or dancing all day in the hot sun, dancing through the night without sleep, or going days without sleeping, and so on. These sacrifices are almost always in a natural environment, except for certain ceremonies taking place in the dead of winter in regions where it is extremely cold, in which case, ceremonies might be held indoors, yet will still involve the sacrifice of fasting and sleep deprivation.

While there are many things taking place in these ceremonies and many derived benefits, the development of physical, mental, and emotional strength is an important benefit that flows from years of practice. It is more of a fringe benefit in a sense that when you have participated in ceremonies for a number of years, you become the kind of person who shrugs off challenges in life that would have previously been devastating or traumatic; you become stronger on all levels.

Developing a willingness and comfort with physical sacrifice in a natural environment provides an opportunity, or to put it more directly, inculcates a compulsion, for experiences with nature in which one connects more directly on a physical level, meaning sleeping on the ground, sitting directly on the ground without ground cover, walking barefoot, hiking to a high place and then sitting for the next four hours in quiet meditation, being willing to be in a really hot or cold environment without being concerned so much about one's physical discomfort, hiking or camping in the rain, or camping far away from a KOA-style restroom or even an outhouse.

These are the kinds of experiences that draw one closer to nature in ways that have a "softening influence," as Luther Standing Bear said, and enable people to experience epiphanies about their lives, gain insights, and most importantly to slow down and be willing to look at life a little differently. These experiences can also offer people an opportunity to measure their own responses to physical discomfort, and in so doing, to come into a deeper recognition of their physical vulnerability and a visceral awareness of their place in nature.

Developing a strong connection to Earth is the starting point for understanding indigenous culture and yet also speaks to the mystical connection of indigenous people from around the world. There is a reason that the only cultures that have lived harmoniously with nature, have lived and thrived for thousands of years with very little shift in culture and little to no deterioration of their standard of living, have without variation practiced religions in which they see all things as being alive, even the rocks, mountains, and Earth herself.

There is a story that speaks to the source of this connection, in which a Native healer is asked about how long it took to figure out what all the healing effects of various plants and roots are, and the healer responded that it didn't take any time at all. "I just spoke to the plants, and they told me what to do." Such experiences are common when there is an openness to what nature may have to teach us.

In my own experience, I have very slowly developed a relationship with fire as a living sentient organism that I can speak with and receive teachings from about my life. On my very first trip to the Navajo reservation in 2001, I found myself at a Sun Dance ceremony, in which I was asked to help watch over the front gate to ensure that people entering the camp did not possess weapons, alcohol, or cameras. In keeping watch, it was necessary to light a fire each evening to keep warm and light while holding vigil until late in the night.

So one evening, just as I was getting ready to build the fire, a group of young Navajo men walked into my camp and sat down to sit and talk, or really more to just sit as they never said much. Being a white guy from Los Angeles, I was rather intimidated about starting a fire with these young Natives watching over. However, I jumped to the task and did my best to build a fire that I thought would take well, took my buck knife and scraped a hunk of pitch from a nearby juniper tree, and gooped it on a couple pieces of brush at the bottom of the pile of wood I had built. Then I lit a match and, poof, the pile of wood took right up.

Then I got cocky and said something rather dumb. "Pretty good for a white boy from Los Angeles, eh?" And just as I said that, the fire sputtered and went out.

The Navajo men said nothing, and neither did they laugh at my stupidity. So then I went back to work, rebuilt the fire, scraped some more pitch, and tried again. And the second time, the same result: poof, the pile of wood caught fire and quickly sputtered and went out.

As I looked at this pile of wood with disappointment and probably showing no small measure of perplexity, one of the young men jumped up to work on the fire while another put his hand on my shoulder and said, "Don't do anything; just watch." The young man pulled a piece of bark from the same juniper tree that I had twice scraped pitch from, twisted the bark into a ball of loose shredded stringlike material, rebuilt the fire to enable a better flow of air, and utilizing the shredded juniper bark had the fire blazing away within three minutes.

I learned several valuable lessons from this experience. Not the least of them was the need for more humility, but more importantly was learning how these young Natives were in relationship with fire. To them, fire was like a friend, an easy relationship that was without mystery or complexity and most importantly that had two sides to the relationship—a give-and-take. They treated the fire with respect, and in turn, the fire provided warmth and light.

To a culture that is not rooted in a connection to Earth, fire will seem like something to control and manipulate, to exploit and to wield. To our modern culture, fire is a tool, a means to an end. To indigenous culture, fire is a relationship.

In our modern world, fire is perceived as an inanimate thing, a mere chemical reaction of air, heat, and fuel, but to the indigenous it is a close friend and companion, and in the context of a ceremonial fire, it becomes a holy deity.

Indigenous people do not treat fire with respect because their elders told them to or because they heard stories about it, and yet both would hold true. They treat fire with respect because they have a living relationship with fire, just as the medicine person who treats ailments with herbs and roots by talking to the plants to receive guidance on which remedies to use for which maladies, or as indigenous people will pray to determine the precise time to plant crops, or pray to ask for rain, or ask permission to take the life of an animal and then use all its parts for food and tools. In all of these examples of such relationships, there is respect and honor.

These relationships, taken as a whole, represent a strong, intrinsic emotional connection to Earth, and when people can cultivate such a relationship, their whole lives will change, and in no small measure so will their approach to business, the decisions they make, the ways in which they communicate, the products they represent, and the ways in which they promote and interact with people. As Luther Standing Bear so eloquently illustrated, a connection to Earth serves to soften a person's heart. Yet this softening influence does not imply a lack of strength, but rather a cultivation of compassion.

At this point in the unfolding of indigenous principles, the reader might be thinking that a solid business executive is one who is strong and disciplined and willing to make tough decisions. This is true, even in the context of this softening influence. This softening does not refer to being wishy-washy, indecisive, or overly emotional.

Indigenous people, and those nonnatives who have lived with and developed a strong connection to Earth, are more willing to experience nature on nature's terms, rather than changing and adapting nature to suit their desire for comfortable experiences. Isn't this on one level what lies at the heart of so much dysfunction in the business world, that there are those who want their work to be comfortable even when there are difficult tasks, challenging conversations, or sticky situations that need to be addressed and resolved? Doesn't avoiding those difficult and sticky situations create a kind of cancer in organizations that can consume them from within?

As an example, when Patagonia ran a full-page ad in the *New York Times* on Black Friday, 2011, with an image of one of their coats and a headline that read "Don't Buy This Jacket,"[1] was it pure marketing genius or complete stupidity brought about by an irrational compulsion to preserve our natural resources? The subheading of the ad, "Common Threads Initiative," followed by "Together we can reduce our environmental footprint" and the simple call to action of "Take the Pledge," served the purpose of cultivating a connection between their products and environmental activism.

Their Common Threads Initiative is a simple pledge to "Reduce, Repair, Reuse, Recycle, and Reimagine.[2] So while many marketing geniuses might have thought Patagonia's CEO, Yvon Chouinard, had lost his marbles, it is important to ask the question, why? Why would they promote their brand in this way?

The same question could be asked of indigenous people as to why they do not believe that a person may own land, that the land belongs to Earth, and that they are just its caretakers. In our modern world, we see land as something to be both enjoyed and exploited. Indigenous people see it as a giant living organism that should be respected. Which is why I've chosen to capitalize Earth, as Indigenous people see her as a living deity.

Perhaps in both these examples, there has been a strong emotional bond created between Earth and people. Indeed, Chouinard spent many years in the outdoors, hiking, climbing, and sleeping on the ground. He certainly had lots of time to contemplate the meaning of Earth and for its softening influence to take effect on his soul.

In our modern world, we go from our air-conditioned homes to our air-conditioned cars to valet park at the gym to exert ourselves on the Stairmaster for forty-five minutes, followed by a hot shower and back into our luxury car brought to us by the valet, and then drive to our covered garage with a connection to our air-conditioned office building. We rely so heavily on air-conditioned environments, central heating, cushy luxury cars, and elegant homes. When do we connect with Earth? When do we give ourselves the opportunity to allow nature to soften our hearts toward Earth? And more importantly, when do we consider Earth in our day-to-day lives, going about all the tasks, projects, and interactions that comprise our time?

If we set aside for a moment the urgent need to dramatically change our environmental practices and simply look at our relationship with Earth from the perspective of how it will affect our lives internally and externally, one could argue that environmental altruism would not have an immediate bearing. Herein lies the core reason for connecting with Earth—not to save Earth, but to *feel* Earth.

The answer, I believe, as to why Chouinard would run an ad campaign telling people not to buy his jacket, or why so many social entrepreneurs are starting businesses left and right to make and sell products that are more environmentally responsible, or why the indigenous do not feel land should be bought and sold, is because they *feel* a connection with Earth.

The transformation in our business dynamics will come into play when we learn to *feel* Earth. We will naturally become more intuitive and less fearful of the future. We will start thinking more long-term, really long-term, and we will be on our way to strengthening other skills like communication, listening, and patience, as we delve into in the coming chapters.

It all begins with Earth.

Chapter 6. Everything Is Alive

Every part of this country is sacred to my people. Every hillside, every valley, every plain and grove has been hallowed by some fond memory or some sad experience of my tribe. Even the rocks, which seem to lie dumb as they swelter in the sun along the silent shore in solemn grandeur, thrill with memories of past events connected with the fate of my people.

–Chief Seattle, Suquamish

Exploring the concept that life exists within all things as a principle for indigenous thinking and culture is closely related to the principle of connection to Earth, as explored in the prior chapter, yet there is a subtle and important distinction.

Beginning in the same place as in chapter 5, with my very first Sun Dance ceremony on the Navajo reservation in 2001, I received a simple and important teaching related to rain. Prior to a long period of drought at this time in 2001, this area of Arizona was still experiencing a monsoon-like type of rain that occurred nearly every afternoon in the summer.

The Sun Dance ceremony takes place in an open arbor and involves dancers who dance throughout the day in the sun for four days without food and water. The ceremony takes place in the middle of summer, when the days are long, hot, and dry. And so for those in support of the dancers, it is always a welcome respite when a quick twenty minutes of hard rain comes in the late afternoon each day to cool the air and quench Earth.

On perhaps the second or third day of the dance when, as always, I was at the front gate keeping vigil, I took refuge under a tarp we had constructed from the back of a truck with a shell, so that we could sit on the tailgate and stay dry from the rain. It was at this time that a young Navajo man approached our camp for a visit.

This young man, however, just stood in the rain despite my invitation to come under the tarp. So instead, I decided to join him. I slid off the tailgate and strolled out to stand next to him. He then told me a story of how it was for him and his siblings as he grew up on this land in northern Arizona. He said each time it would rain, his father would go into their family hogan and gather up all the kids to come out in the rain. He explained to his children to always be grateful for the rain, to come out and greet it and acknowledge the blessing that it is, as it nourishes Earth and provides for all that they have.

At this point in my journey, I had already spent a good number of years learning to enjoy nature on nature's terms, yet I was still a city boy in nature. This was just another small step in the direction of understanding how much wealth of knowledge can come from experiencing nature on its own terms.

How many times in our business lives have we experienced disappointment or defeat and later discovered that those disappointments were exactly what we needed so that other things could come into being that are even better than our original vision? How many times have we heard people describing the rain in pejorative terms like, "The weather is terrible today," or "It's an ugly day today"? How many times have we heard the rain described as a blessing?

When we experience disappointment in our businesses, are we caved in, depressed, angry, or frustrated; or do we look for the blessing, perhaps the wisdom, in the turn of events? Many great business thinkers of today and of the past have spoken about the need for businesses to inculcate a culture that fosters creativity by allowing people to make mistakes, as it is from our mistakes that we learn and grow. John F. Kennedy once said, "Those who dare to fail miserably can achieve greatly."[1] Gandhi wrote, "Heroes are made in the hour of defeat. Success is, therefore, well described as a series of glorious defeats."[2] And Henry Ford said, "Even a mistake may turn out to be the one thing necessary to a worthwhile achievement."[3]

To continue with lessons that come from water, it is important to note that water plays a central role in nearly every ceremony in every indigenous culture everywhere on Earth. Rain is a form of water, and to indigenous people, it is not inanimate. It is not a simple molecule made up of two parts hydrogen and one part oxygen. It is a living thing.

In 2003 at the end of one of my trips to the Navajo reservation, my adopted family asked me to help them with the drought they had been experiencing for the prior two years. They had livestock for which they were hauling water, they had corn they were growing, and their community at large was suffering from a severe lack of rain that began in 2002. So on my last night with the family as I was getting ready to leave for home in Los Angeles, they decided to send with me some sacred medicines that belong to their family and instruct me in a ceremony to perform at the ocean's edge that would bring rain to their land.

The next morning, the father of the family got up long before sunrise and drove to the land where their livestock were held to collect some of these medicines. By the time I got up at 5:00 a.m., the whole family was awake in the living room ready to begin the ritual of selecting these medicines and apportioning them to me. A white cloth was laid down, and each person in the family went and selected sacred stones one by one and placed them in the cloth. The cloth was folded in a very specific manner, and I was instructed in a very specific manner how to unfold and how to perform the ceremony at the ocean in Southern California.

Several days later, just before sunrise on a stretch of beach just north of Los Angeles, I released these medicines into the ocean. I cannot divulge the details of the ceremony itself as it would not be appropriate to do so, but what I can say is that what I experienced was incredibly profound. It was exactly as if the ocean were a living thing and expressed hunger for these medicines. It was as if the ocean were saying, "Hurry up. I'm ready to take what you have." A group of dolphins popped up swimming around just a short way in front of me, and a single solitary seagull landed in front of me and walked a perfect clockwise circle around me as I prepared to release the medicines.

The drought did not end at that time, yet on that day in the summer of 2003, it rained in northern Arizona.

It was explained to me that hundreds of years ago, the Navajo people made journeys to the ocean. They brought offerings for the ocean, and they brought things home with them, one of which was the water itself, the water of the ocean. They see the ocean as a very sacred thing, and seawater itself is a powerful medicine. It was also explained to me how I could bring water from the ocean out to the reservation for the benefit of the land and the people there. They explained how I was to make an offering, say a prayer, and harvest water in an intentional way, which is what I began doing the following summer.

The first time I brought seawater to Navajo country, I picked up my adopted Navajo brother Daniel in a little-known town called Tolani Lake, Arizona. We drove to the far eastern side of the reservation to one of the four sacred mountains of the Navajo people called Dzilth-Na-O-Dith-Hle (don't try and pronounce it, as it will tongue twist all but the Navajo people themselves), or DZ for short. We were there to take part in a ceremony, actually a grouping of ceremonies all taking place simultaneously on one night.

We began with a sweat-lodge ceremony, which entails heating large rocks in a fire until they are glowing red and bringing those hot stones into a lodge, a small enclosure that snugly holds eight to ten people sitting on the ground around a small pit in which the rocks are placed, a door is closed, water is poured on the stones to produce steam, and we sing and pray. (For more on the sweat-lodge ceremony, see chapter 16.) However, in this ceremony, my brother Daniel poured some of the seawater I brought into a bucket mixed with water from DZ. So in this ceremony on this occasion, we were pouring seawater from Southern California, harvested in an intentional manner and brought with prayers for rain to this small community in New Mexico, an area that many would consider to be desolate, largely devoid of trees, and at this time in the middle of the summer, very hot and very dry.

When we crawled into this lodge, there was not a cloud in the sky. We closed the door after the rocks were brought in, my brother Daniel spoke for a while, and then he began singing and pouring water on the stones. The moment he started pouring water, we heard thunder clapping outside, and in short order the rain began to pour. Inside the lodge, it was extremely hot. Outside the land was being cooled off. It poured that whole first round, and the moment Daniel stopped pouring and asked for the door to be opened, the rain stopped.

I crawled out, rejuvenated the fire, and brought more rocks in for a second round in the lodge. Again we closed the door, Daniel shared a few words, and he started singing and pouring water. Again it began to pour outside as Daniel poured seawater on the hot rocks. The moment he stopped pouring and we opened the door, signaling the end of the second round, it stopped raining. This repeated again in the third round and again in the fourth and final round of the sweat ceremony. Within minutes of us coming out from the lodge, the sky was clear and blue again.

Then that evening as we began the tepee ceremonies, we utilized the seawater once again. The tepee ceremonies—four of them running concurrently—began at dusk and ended shortly after sunrise. At the halfway point in the evening, there is what is referred to as the midnight water ceremony. It was at this time that the seawater was utilized and spilled on the ground. There was a medicine man who spoke words about the seawater and what it meant to their people, and there was a request for people to pray for rain. In all, it was a beautiful ceremony, as they always are out there in this desert land known as DZ and revered as a sacred site. The next day, there was much socializing and a big feast. Then we took the tepees down, everyone cleaned up, and we all drove home.

An e-mail went out a couple of weeks later from the medicine man that had organized the ceremony to those who came from great distances, to let us know that it had rained for eight days after we left.

If one spends enough time in and around indigenous ceremonies, one will experience many miracles like this and others. Yet I am not suggesting that we all seek out our local Indian and ask for a miracle; rather, I am suggesting that the miracle exists everywhere and that the potential for creating miracles exists in each one of us.

For those who look at life and nature from a purely materialistic standpoint consisting of chemical reactions, evolutionary biology, and randomness, nature seems as though it is an unpredictable random force. And in such terms, nature is therefore something that we need to study and figure out how to control. We must change the course of rivers, create lakes, move mountains, clear forests, create energy systems, drill for water, and develop a society that is completely insulated from this unpredictable force.

To the indigenous, it is all one big blessing to give thanks for, and when it is really cold or really dry or any way that makes life hard, they give thanks and ask for the elements—the thunder beings, the water of life, the deities of Fire, Air, and Earth—to help them with their needs.

How would we manage our businesses differently if we left our fear of the unknown aside and learned to trust that all is alive and that we are but a piece of the collective whole, fully enabled to communicate with that which seems unknowable? Perhaps we would operate with a powerful sense of calm confidence, knowing that there is no challenge we cannot overcome, no unknown that we cannot reconcile, no imbalance that we cannot right, and that ultimately we do not need to attempt to control anything, only seek to fulfill our creative desires and flow with the collective whole in a way that is extremely fun and fulfilling for all.

More recently I was at a sobriety powwow in Cherokee, North Carolina, where I was sitting on the drum, in this case, the only drum as it was a very small powwow with just a hundred or so people. Sitting on the drum means that I was one of up to eight or so men sitting around a large-sized drum, each of us drumming in unison and singing the traditional powwow songs.

We had just sung for the grand entry when it began to rain, at first a sprinkle, then a downpour. The tradition of grand entry is to sing a grand-entry song as the dancers dance clockwise into the arena, then there is a prayer from an elder, then a flag song, then we post the flags, then an honor song, and then we begin the powwow. Yet before we could begin the flag and honor songs, everyone ran for cover as the rain was really coming down.

Fortunately the drum group I was sitting with, together with the sound system and the emcee, was under a canopy. The emcee, who was also an elder, had checked the weather forecast that morning and announced that the forecast was calling for rain on and off throughout the day. At that moment, another elder, who was also the lead singer of the drum I was sitting on, turned to the emcee and said, "If we don't acknowledge these thunder beings, they're going to keep raining on us." When he said this, a couple of the women dancers overheard and chorused the sentiment. There was an immediate suggestion for us to keep singing, which is what we did. The emcee looked confused, yet went along with it.

We started another song with the dancers and spectators huddled under trees and umbrellas. We sang real hard to let the thunder beings know that we acknowledged and appreciated them, and by the end of the song, the rain had stopped and held until just after the powwow ended that evening.

The elder emcee was thinking in materialist terms. The elder lead singer was rooted in the aliveness of all things. To the elder lead singer, the rain was a joyous thing.

The materialist business executive will say things like, "We need to always be focused on the bottom line." The executive who acknowledges the aliveness of all things will say, "We need to always be focused on our customer experience, the quality of our product, the happiness of our employees, and the integrity of our decisions." The materialist will own a publishing company and think that revenue is the most important.

The aliveness leader will own a publishing company and get excited about the amazing content that is being delivered. The materialist will own a computer company and focus on consistently lowering labor and materials costs; the aliveness leader will focus on the user experience.

Steve Jobs was a fine example of an aliveness leader. He said back in 1985,

> We think the Mac will sell zillions, but we didn't build the Mac for anybody else. We built it for ourselves. We were the group of people who were going to judge whether it was great or not. We weren't going to go out and do market research. We just wanted to build the best thing we could build. When you're a carpenter making a beautiful chest of drawers, you're not going to use a piece of plywood on the back, even though it faces the wall and nobody will ever see it. You'll know it's there, so you're going to use a beautiful piece of wood on the back. For you to sleep well at night, the aesthetic, the quality, has to be carried all the way through.[4]

In chapter 5, we explored the lessons that come from developing a strong connection to Earth: that we become more intuitive and that we think more long-term and begin to lessen the bonds of fear that come from being disconnected from Earth. In chapter 6, we have delved to a deeper level of moving beyond fear, that we can really sense and feel a connection to all things animate and inanimate, that there is no unknown that we cannot connect with and appeal to. We can now delve into our work and our lives with a childlike gust and passion for adventure, shedding the need for control and manipulation, working in common for a common good and enjoying the heck out of it in the process.

These lessons may seem subtle, or perhaps not, depending on the perspective of the reader, yet it is important to consider that these principles build upon one another; to take any one or two by themselves will have a minimal impact on leadership. Rather, if we can consider these principles both individually and holistically, we can begin to see a profound effect on our ability to lead organizations in a meaningful way.

I have heard it said over and over how nature is a storehouse of information far greater than any library or learning institution. So it is through developing a deep connection with Earth and seeing the aliveness of all things that we can catapult our learning to a whole new level. This is the foundation of all indigenous culture and understanding. In order for one to garner the wisdom of this culture, it is necessary to start here, with more than a mere appreciation for nature—with a visceral bond and connection to all life and all of its systems.

Chapter 7. The Elders

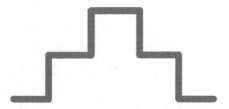

When you get older and you are ready, your ancestors will show up to guide you.

—Joe Coyhis, Stockbridge-Munsee

Knowledge is a beautiful thing, but the use of knowledge in a good way is what makes for wisdom. Learning how to use knowledge in a sacred manner, that's wisdom to me. And to me, that's what a true Elder is.

—Sun Bear, Chippewa

A Cayuga elder tells a story of a village elder who sat in a seat of wisdom. The people came to this elder to ask all sorts of questions, and never was there a time when he could not provide an answer. This elder had a grandson who coveted the position that his grandfather held, and so one day said to his grandfather that he would like to sit in his chair and answer the questions brought by the people.

The grandfather said to his grandson that if he could ask him a question that he, Grandfather, could not answer, the grandson would be able to take his place. The grandson, being crafty as he was, sought out a bird's nest, from which he reached in and grabbed a small bird. He then approached his grandfather with the bird concealed in his hand behind his back.

He then told his grandfather that he held a bird in his hand and asked the old man whether it was dead or alive. The young man thought that if his grandfather said the bird was alive, he would squeeze it and show him a dead bird, and if he said it was dead, he would show him the bird alive. Either way, he would prove the old man wrong.

After a moment of consideration, the boy's grandfather responded, "Whether the bird lives or dies, it will be up to you."

This is a simple and enjoyable story illustrating the value and wisdom of the elders, and also the great esteem in which indigenous people hold their elders. This again is very consistent from one end of the globe to the other among indigenous people.

In our modern world of fast-moving technology, communications systems, and ever expanding global trade, there is a tendency to discount the value of elders, as they are viewed as without value to the culture of today. Indeed, I can say of my twenty-year-old daughter, who is pursuing a career in social media and leans heavily toward right-brain thinking, that she seems to grasp new software, apps, and computer technology with great alacrity, far more rapidly than I, as more of a left-brain thinker, am able to do. It is as though the generation of teens and twenties—regardless of their creative or analytical leanings—are hardwired for technology and generally seem to be frustrated with how slow those of us in our forties, fifties, and older seem to be toward technology. Yet principles hold true for a society regardless of its technology, the current style of clothing, or who the latest pop singer is.

The concept of elders in indigenous culture is less about how much gray hair people possess or their chronological age, and more about the way they live their lives, the compassion of their hearts, and the wisdoms they share. Being an elder comes from having lived a life, in most cases a long life, in strict adherence to a set of principles that defines indigenous culture, which when practiced consistently and persistently brings about a deep inculcation of all of these principles explored in this book and many more.

Being an elder in the indigenous sense is also about becoming a servant to the people. In essence they have given their lives over to the rearing of wisdom within their society, which includes dispensing healing remedies, praying for people who are in need of help, offering guidance in decision making, and serving as a living embodiment of a human being with a fully open and compassionate heart.

Elders do not harbor resentments. They do not envy others or covet their possessions. They do not speak often, yet when they do, their words carry an uncommon power to direct attention, cut through confusion, and strike to the heart of things that block forward movement. They do not argue. They listen mostly and speak only when they have something of value to share, and most importantly, they are humble in ways that are of great significance. The Navajo people have a most beautiful way of referring to those who have achieved a true state of elder-hood; they refer to them as those who "walk in beauty."

In one ceremony, a tepee ceremony, in which I was holding the position of cedarman, I had a quick and powerful lesson in the kind of humility that true elders possess. The cedarman, or in some cases cedarwoman, is one who dispenses cedar on the coals of the fire for the benefit of all those in the ceremony. The cedarman is a helper to anyone who may be struggling in the ceremony and is also asked to share a few words of wisdom at two specific points of the ceremony. The cedarman also sits to the left of the roadman, the person running the ceremony. In this ceremony, the roadman was a Lakota elder, a very wise man and a chief to his people.

At some point during the ceremony, roughly around two in the morning, the roadman went out for a short restroom break. It was at this time that I had a question to ask of him related to a formality I was requesting for the sponsor of the ceremony. Rather than allowing him to take his seat first and then ask the question, I eagerly blurted it out just as he was to pass in front of me on his way to taking his seat. My eagerness threw him a bit, and he thought I was asking him not to pass in front of me.

This created a rather awkward situation for me, as there I had an elder, a hugely wise and humble elder, a chief among his people, standing there thinking he had just committed some breach of protocol and asking me what I needed him to do. Once I realized the confusion, I smiled and said, "Oh, sorry. Please come by. I would never try and tell you what to do." And I motioned for him to pass.

The truly stunning thing about this is that his humble response was instant. It was not premeditated, and it showed to me that this way of being is core to who he is. How incredibly compelling this struck me as being that a man of his years, experience, and knowledge rose not to a level of entitlement, but rather a level of service and humility.

There are those who call themselves elders, and I have met at least a couple who relish the esteem in which they are held and exhibit pride in their knowledge. And then there are those as this elder, whom I have learned volumes from, as he is the kind of person I aspire to be. In light of this elder, how can I ever become too confident in my knowledge and wisdom to think that I have nothing further to learn?

Herein lies a significant and compelling reason for us to value our elders—the examples they set. By having lived a life of meaning and purpose, elders become meaningful and purposeful in their example. Just as we admire great accomplishments of an Olympic athlete, a professional opera singer, a virtuoso musician, or a great writer of fiction, elders are our virtuosos of life, eschewing selfishness, embracing holism, embodying compassion, and demonstrating love. They walk in beauty.

Of course I am not suggesting that all elders possess equal wisdom and consistently embody uncompromised examples of virtue. There is a mind-set in the business world that often says, "We must change or die"; such a directive is often interpreted to mean, "Ignore the past." Many times reorganizations result in new people in new positions with new ideas, or so they think. Often new ideas are not so new, as they have been tried before. Yet if we do not honor the elders in our organizations and their experience, we are quite likely to repeat the mistakes of the past.

By elders in our organizations, I am not referring just to those with lots of gray hair, but to those with ten, fifteen, twenty years, or more with a company, as these are the individuals who have seen the changes over time, the successful strategies, the failed strategies, the positive attributes, and the areas of dysfunction. Even the failures have great value if we will only be willing to look at them honestly and completely. Many times successful strategies will fail due to bad execution, and sometimes strategies that are less than perfect will succeed because the people behind them did whatever they had to do to make them successful. Yet we will never know these things about our prior strategies if we do not listen to our elders and be willing to really hear what they have to say.

In my first year with the big-city newspaper, I was working on the launch of a new conference, for which we hired a retired event professional as a consultant to assist us with the project. In this case, the consultant had a lot of gray hair; he had started and built several event companies, sold the last one, and was living a rather comfortable retirement from the proceeds of the sale.

I noticed right away how confidently he spoke in meetings. He seemed to have the ability to project the future results of strategies that were being discussed with an incredible authoritativeness, and as a result, some in the company disliked him intensely as they did not like their ideas being shot down. For the most part, he did not seem to hold any emotional investment in whether people followed his advice, yet to the extent that we did follow his advice, things seemed to work quite nicely.

Right away I made the decision to befriend this consultant and attempt to learn all that I could from him, which proved to be a highly valuable decision as many of his teachings benefited my work in the event business for years to come. Even as technology changed rapidly through the late nineties and early 2000s, the principles I learned from him related to selling events and organizational systems held true, and still do to this day. While our styles are quite different, I learned certain fundamental principles in less than a year of working with this consultant that might have otherwise taken me ten years or more to learn through my own direct experience.

It is also interesting to note that in my present consulting work, I often find myself working with those in their twenties and early thirties, young entrepreneurs with great passion and energy, yet lacking many highly necessary basic understandings and skill sets required to build successful companies. For example, finance seems to be an area that many young entrepreneurs seem to lack the patience for. They would rather leave the finances to an accountant, hire someone like me to write their business plan, and then charge ahead launching businesses and stumbling along through the process when confronted with the complexities of HR requirements, operating financial models, staffing structure, client contract terms, debt management, and so on.

Many organizations value the energy and enthusiasm of younger executives over the meditative and methodical approach of older executives, and may tend to hire an entire team of twenty-somethings with the intent of obtaining more productivity and passion per person. What if a young tech company retained one elder on the team, a person of significant business experience and success, maybe even someone who did not fully get the technology of the company, and then all this elder contributed was one word of wisdom per week, would the elder not be worth his or her weight in gold?

What if that one word of wisdom helped people to think differently, avert obvious mistakes, or serve as a steady example of effective and respectful communication? What if that elder did not even work a full week? Maybe that would be a way of obtaining a person of such experience at a salary roughly equivalent to other high-level executives in the company. Perhaps the elder would not need to work a full week to stay plugged in and evaluate strategies and practices. Elders could mentor the younger executives who desire it to help them to grow into powerhouse leaders in the organization. They could evaluate systems top to bottom. They could meet with bankers, negotiate vendor deals, coach the sales team, and continuously offer big-picture perspectives. Would such a team member not be significantly valuable?

In that very same ceremony described earlier in this chapter in which I was sitting in the cedar position with an elder roadman running the ceremony, there was another great learning I received. At a key point in the ceremony, he gave some very specific guidance to the sponsor of the ceremony, which I felt at the time not to be what the sponsor needed. The way in which the elder was advising this man seemed contrary to all my experience and training of more than fifteen years of attending tepee ceremonies. The elder also barely knew the sponsor, while he was a close friend of mine, someone I knew extremely well.

Yet the morning after the ceremony, the wisdom of this guidance became clear to me, and then a month later more clear, and then three months later more clear, and then six months later it became crystal clear. It took as long as six months for me to come into a full appreciation for the incredible wisdom in the guidance this elder provided. It was, in fact, pristinely perfect for this specific person at this specific time in his life. While I cannot share the specific teaching itself as it would be too personal, I can say that I believe the sponsor to this day remains in appreciation of this wisdom.

If I had been impatient in this ceremony and discounted this teaching as coming from some older man who was no longer in tune with the times, I would have missed a huge lesson. My fifteen years of experience and intensive training in these ceremonial ways still did not stack up even close to this elder's wisdom. How much more I have to learn, how much I appreciate these elders, is so significant. What I have been able to take from this indigenous principle of respecting and honoring the elders into the business world has been hugely beneficial to my work.

Indeed, we need passion and energy in our lives and our work. We also need youthfulness and at times playfulness, and yet in order to achieve success on a scale that brings our lives into a place of meaning and purpose, we also need to balance our youthfulness with the wisdom of the elders. Elders will tell us this as well, that they themselves can at times be playful and youthful, which presents us with an important point of transition into the next chapter, "The Four Directions," and the concept of universal balance.

Chapter 8. The Four Directions

When faithful human beings or other creatures called upon them
for help, they [the powers of the four directions] must send their
powers ...

—Fools Crow, Lakota

Each of the four directions has special powers. These powers or
Grandfathers are there to help us. The powers are from the East,
the South, the West, and the North. To call upon the power we
need to stand in the center and face each of the directions and
honor all forms of life in each direction. Facing the East we honor
all the two legged, four legged, winged ones, plants' nation and
the animals. We repeat this prayer in each of the four directions.
This allows us to become centered. When we are centered, then we
are ready to call the helpers. It is said, when the student is ready,
the teacher appears. If we are to be ready, we need to remember

to always get quiet first. We do this by honoring and praying to the four directions.

—Elder's Meditation, June 26, 2012[1]

In every indigenous ceremony I have experienced, there has always been a calling in, or an honoring or recognition, of the four directions, sometimes with a song or series of songs, sometimes with an offering of cornmeal or tobacco, or sometimes with a prayer and the blowing of an eagle-bone whistle. The concept of the four directions is so fundamental to indigenous thinking that it is engrained into every level of their society, philosophy, and religion. The four directions also hold many meanings for indigenous people, complementary meanings held together as one cohesive principle: that all things happen in fours—the four seasons; the four races of red, black, yellow, and white; the four ages of human life as defined by the Mayan calendar system and the Hopi prophesies; the four elements of water, air, fire, and Earth; the four quadrants of the medicine wheel, represented by red, black, yellow, and white; and most importantly, the spirits of the four directions that come when called upon.

In May 2007, a few hours after midnight in a tepee ceremony in the Southern California desert, I had a life-changing moment. For the sake of the agnostic readers, you could say a moment of great clarity; for those who can accept the presence of a higher power, I would say that God spoke to me and proclaimed very clearly and rather insistently, "Now is your time."

I knew immediately what this meant. It was time for me to sponsor a tepee ceremony for myself, as at that point, I had spent nine years in these ceremonies and had not yet sponsored a ceremony. I had been feeling for some time that it was becoming time. I just needed a sign, a catalyzing moment of clarity to push me over the fence of indecision and procrastination. I needed for Spirit to be extremely insistent, to not take no for an answer, and make it abundantly clear what I needed to do.

At this time, except for the work I was doing with the ceremonies, my life had become stagnant on every level. I was progressing in my understanding of indigenous culture and religion, and as a result, was changing gradually and continuously on an internal level. Yet all of the outward aspects of my life had remained largely unchanged. I had grown tired of those external attributes; I had evolved beyond the current container of my life and desperately needed change. I needed to break out in new directions and experience new things.

So the path I needed to take had been made abundantly clear. I needed to call for a ceremony and ask the Great Spirit for massive life change.

"Massive?" a sister in the community questioned. "Are you sure you want to use the word massive?"

"Yes," I replied. "It's what I really want."

And so it was.

In chapter 10, I'll go into more detail related to the preparation of this ceremony, as it relates so keenly to the indigenous principle of intentionality. For now, I will simply say a little of the result.

Within a week of this ceremony, which was held on August 4, 2007, my now former wife and I made the decision to separate. Within seven weeks, we were separated. This was massive life change number one, the ending of a nineteen-year marriage. To clarify, I am not suggesting that spiritual and emotional progression should mean the ending of marriages, only that in my case I had grown beyond the nature of my marriage and it was no longer healthy for me.

Within weeks of the ceremony, I received what seemed like a random call from a man who wanted the newspaper to be a media sponsor of an event he was producing. When I met this man, I immediately liked him, and his vision resonated with me in a significant way. So while I was not typically the person at the paper to negotiate media sponsorships, I took this one and ran with it. I pushed the deal through to provide him the media exposure necessary to ensure that his event would be a success, and it was. It also proved to be a good brand experience for the paper as well. This relationship led to a meeting with the president of a boutique event company that exclusively produces sustainability-related events out of western North Carolina, and this meeting led to me being recruited by this company. Massive life change number two was leaving the paper, moving to North Carolina, and shifting the direction of my career.

One year and three months after moving to North Carolina, I met my present wife, a woman of uncommon compassion and wisdom, and found with her a level of compatibility, trust, and love that I had not previously thought possible between a man and a woman—massive life change number three.

Then in December 2009, I was out visiting in Southern California for a ceremony with my So Cal ceremony community and was expressing to the man who conducted the ceremony that set these changes in motion the gratitude I had for these three massive life changes. His response was, "Well, everything comes in fours."

This gave me reason for pause, a very significant pause, as each of the prior three changes were scary, and the first two rather hard. Yet I sensed immediately what the fourth change would be—that it would be related to my work.

Three months later, it began to become apparent that I was in conflict with the direction in which the company I was working for was going. I could no longer be in complete support of the ownership of the company and needed to leave, which led to massive life change number four, to let go of the concept of having a job and become an independent consultant.

The lesson in this story is multidimensional. Without even knowing what specific changes I wanted in my life, I knew I wanted to leave my job and California; I did not yet know what other changes were necessary in my life in order to come to a place of peace and wholeness. What I did was call for a ceremony, a ceremony that called to the four directions, in which we had four sacred smokes, after which I observed four days of reverence, and over the next four years received four big life changes.

If I had asked for just one or maybe two life changes, I would still be in a relative state of unhappiness. If I had been too specific in how I wanted my life to be, I would have cheated myself out of an adventure far greater than I was capable of imagining for myself.

In business, anytime we constrict our objectives to just one thing or a few things that we think are necessary for our success, then we are robbing ourselves and our companies of the grand adventure that could befall us. The most glaring example is when we place profitability above all other objectives. We say we need to focus on the bottom line because we won't have a company if we are not profitable. When we do this, we are ignoring other equally important objectives that all successful companies require in order to be in a state of prosperity. We do not have a company without suppliers, employees, clients, customers, and a community that is in support of us. We also will not have a biosphere that will comfortably support human life if we do not also think of the environment and seek to be in balance with it.

It is actually more than just that these other objectives are important; they are integral. When we drive our businesses with a narrow focus, we are in essence consuming some of our assets to support others, and this construct can only survive for a limited period of time before difficult upheaval will thrust itself upon us. For example, driving employees too hard until they burn out, quit, and take institutional knowledge with them; pushing so hard on suppliers that they lose respect and stop doing all they can do for us; driving so hard for greater revenue from our clients so that we lose their loyalty; or disregarding the need for balance in our community and losing its respect for our company and what we do.

Indigenous people do not acknowledge the four directions because of custom or ritual. They acknowledge the powers of an integral system of life that works best when they work in concert with the whole. They see themselves as a component of a greater whole, and when they appeal to the four directions, they are in balance and they are centered. If, for example, when holding ceremony they only called to three of the four directions, they would be cheating themselves out of all that their lives could be. In this example, they would also be disrespecting that one direction that was left out, and their lives would be out of balance.

In addition to being a principle, the concept of the four directions is also a mind-set and a practice. It is a way of relating to the world, a way of honoring all the diversity that exists, and a way of seeing oneself as a piece in a greater dynamic system of interdependent components consisting of people, places, things, animals, elements, and Spirit or higher power. It is a deeper way of relating to life, as it takes the focus off oneself and expands it outward in an infinite arch of understanding.

It also explains a little of why the Natives of the colonial days did not understand the European concept of owning land; they did not see themselves in such a light as to have dominion over the land and the natural elements. So, sure, they would receive a few trinkets, a few blankets and beads, and mark an "X" on a piece of paper so the white settlers would think they owned the land. They thought this to be silly, and so at first did not take it seriously.

The concept of the triple bottom line (people, planet, and profits) is a giant leap forward in expanding our sense of interdependencies, yet the concept is still missing a fourth necessary objective, the objective of purpose. One could say that purpose is implied in people, as people are most happy when they feel purposeful, yet one could also suggest that profits is also a people-oriented objective, as we feel good when we are prosperous.

I think the most significant insight we can take from the indigenous principle of the four directions is that purpose is important for the sake of all other objectives. It is why indigenous ceremonies are intensely purposeful in all that they do. There is no self-interest involved in living one's life in acknowledgement of the interconnected nature of all things; it is simply the way things are, and when we discover this, we learn how to live our lives more purposefully. If we could adopt the collective objectives of people, planet, profits, and purpose, we would be closer to collective prosperity, balance with nature, fulfillment in work, and meaning in our lives.

Chapter 9. Patience

You have to have a lot of patience to hear those old people talk, because when they talk, they talk about motivation, the feeling, the unsound that is around the universe. They explain everything to one understanding. They bring it all together, and when they finish, just one word comes out. Just one word. They might talk all day, and just one word comes out.

—Wallace Black Elk, Lakota

Adopt the pace of nature: her secret is patience.

—Ralph Waldo Emerson

Patience has been a very hard lesson for me. At one point in time, you could almost say that I celebrated my impatience in that I had accepted it as an inherent characteristic of my personality and even shared it openly so people would know this about me. While I essentially wanted everything to happen yesterday, I have also always been extremely thorough and not prone to cutting corners. This meant that I always worked twice as hard as a good portion of my colleagues, and also that I was always under a great deal of self-driven stress, constantly teetering on the verge of burnout.

For the majority of my time participating in indigenous ceremonies, I would become painfully aware of my impatience almost immediately from the point of arriving at ceremony grounds, as the pace of things around ceremonies is decidedly slower than the world of city life. I had the same feeling upon entering the more remote areas of the Navajo reservation, as the style of communication of most indigenous people tends to be slower, more deliberate, and even meditative.

In my adopted Navajo family, I have many relations; and my first stop on the reservation has always been my now late sister Pauline's home in Leupp, Arizona, a small community some forty-five miles outside of Flagstaff. Pauline passed away unexpectedly in January of 2014. Prior to her passing I would only get to see her once or twice a year, I was always excited to see her, and after spending many hours in a car prior to arriving at her home, I had the tendency to burst with conversation.

Pauline would just sit and listen and say little to nothing. Then after ten minutes or so, when I realized that I was talking too much, I would slow down and just sit. Pauline never seemed to have a problem with just sitting with someone without conversation, even if it's been a long time since being with this relative.

Then after twenty minutes or so, she would begin to speak. At that time and very fortunately for me, I would have the good sense to just listen. As her gait was extremely slow and deliberate, nothing in what she spoke of was incidental or trivial. I always found great meaning in her words, yet I was only able to grasp her meaning if I was able to slow down and match her cadence.

After about a half day on the reservation, or within twenty minutes of arriving at ceremony grounds, I would become aware of a subtle internal feeling, almost physical in nature as it felt centered in my chest cavity, in which I would feel this grating feeling as if sandpaper were slowly rubbing on my internal organs. It was a physical manifestation of an emotional and mental impatience with the slow pace of things. My meter wanted to get going with everything now. However, in these environments, we do not use clocks, watches, or iPhones. Here we're on Indian time, which means things will happen when they happen and people will speak when they have something to say and not a minute before.

If I were to have given way to this impatience and allowed it to manifest in the form of questions about when things are happening or suggestions to initiate something, it would have been as if I were speaking another language to my indigenous relations. They would just sit there, maybe say nothing, maybe crack a joke, or maybe change the subject. It simply wouldn't compute with their way of being.

After a few days on the reservation or by midway through a ceremony, I would have slowed down, relaxed, matched cadence with the melodic Navajo-speaking indigenous ones, and the internal grating feeling in my chest cavity would have dissipated. And yet, upon my next trip to the reservation or my next time at ceremony, the process would repeat, as once I returned to my big city and my corporate job, I would slip right back into my typical pace of living and working. I would have to slow down all over again.

Beginning in 2007 and lasting for at least a year, nearly every time I arrived at ceremony grounds and within five minutes of arriving, I would seriously whack my left shin in exactly the same place. I would whack it so hard that it would welt up and remain sore for the next week and a half.

One time I pulled up and saw people pulling wood off a pile and carrying it over near the fire, splitting and stacking it ready for use. So I parked and quickly scurried up on the pile of wood to select pieces and carry them over. The moment I got up on the pile of wood, I stepped on one piece with my right foot in such a way that it flipped up and whacked my left shin. Another time I was entering someone's house in the dark, and just as someone said, "Be careful; there's a hole in the floor over there," I stepped in the hole and whacked my shin in the same place. Yet another instance: I went to hop up onto a truck bed to pull wood out, slipped, and landed on the edge of the tail bed on my left shin. And yet another time, I grabbed an ax, swung it at a piece of wood, and instead of connecting solidly, it ricocheted off and hit me in—well, you get the idea.

The lesson for me was that I was bringing a fast and chaotic pace of doing things into an environment that is all about connecting with the spirit world, which is a world that is not based on linear time, to-do lists, or action plans. My energy and pace were in conflict with such a realm, and after a good number of years of immersion in this culture and religion, it was as if Spirit would no longer accept this energy from me, and so decided to make the lesson more physically painful so I would get the message. I got the message. (For more on the spirit world, see chapter 16.)

More recently, in the fall of 2011 right after coming out of an all-night tepee ceremony, something really important became exceedingly clear to me. In the religion of tepee ceremonies, we utilize instruments, which refers to drums, gourd rattles, drum sticks, and fans made of feathers fixed with a handle and fringe. Most people who take on this religion will go to great lengths to obtain a fan made of feathers within their first year or two. In my case, I had spent more than fourteen years in the religion and still had not gotten around to completing this process.

One can purchase these instruments, but this is not the traditional way and not the way I wanted to do it. One could commission someone to make a fan for him or her, and while I had considered this for a number of years, I never quite felt right about this method either. As these instruments are utilized for the purpose of extending, guiding, and enhancing our prayers, the way I was taught was that we make our own instruments so they posses all our own thoughts and prayers imbued into every fiber of their construction.

The problem with that—and the reason why it took me fourteen years to get around to making a fan—is that I never saw myself as a craftsperson and frankly was terrified at the concept of having to spend long hours carefully and methodically cutting, stitching, gluing, and beading. Neither did I have much confidence in my visual skills to create a fan that would actually be beautiful. I felt that I was not cut out for this type of work.

Yet the strong awareness that came over me on this brisk morning in the fall of 2011 was that it was now time for me to make a fan. I had been gifted with the right kind of feathers some six years earlier and even halfheartedly began constructing a fan with them some two years prior, but then got busy and stopped. I had been counseled numerous times that one does not start making a fan and then not finish, or leave feathers in an unfinished state, as it reflects on our lives as having important, unfinished business. I flew across the country two times for ceremony with the intention of passing these feathers to a brother of mine in the community to ask him to construct a fan for me. The work of this brother is superb. As he is also a medicine person, I would have felt very comfortable having him make an instrument of prayer for me. Yet both times, either some odd occurrence prevented me from seeing him or I totally forgot to pass the feathers to him when we saw each other.

The message was clear. This would be an assignment for me, and there would be a lesson to learn. I had some strong inner knowing that the making of this fan would be connected to my life in general, that it would not just be about carving out time and slogging through it to see a project to completion, but that this would change me in some way.

For the better part of the next two months, I spent countless hours crafting, working with feathers, leather, thread, and beads. I set my insecurities aside related to my visual skills and burned sage while I worked, listened to the music of the tepee ceremonies, and placed myself in a meditative state while progressing my way through the construction of this fan.

As I had never made a fan before, I also needed a teacher and asked my good brother Whoosh Kaalii, also on the other side of the country, if he would help. Whoosh Kaalii is like me, a man of mostly European descent who came into the Native ways with a deep abiding commitment to learn the traditional ways as carefully as possible, except his time in these ways was at least twice my own and he is a man of true craftsmanship and artistry.

Whoosh Kaalii grew up on a hunting and cattle ranch in the Big Horn Mountains of Wyoming, so his connection to Earth came at an early age as he spent the better part of nine months of the year in the outdoors. He is also a jack of many trades in constructing things, building, painting, digital arts, and of course, crafting.

I held many Skype calls with Whoosh Kaalii in which I was able to show him my work and gain critical guidance throughout the process. Our conversations would start with the technical details related to the construction of the fan, and many times would migrate to the elements of my life that the creation of the fan was related to. He was a tough teacher, at times suggesting that I take things apart that I had spent many hours, sometimes days, putting together because it was not quite right. He would continually remind me not to be in a hurry, to take as much time as I needed to get it right, and to consider the fan as a reflection of my life. My progress was slow.

Throughout the process of making this fan, I felt that familiar subtle grating feeling on my internal organs, that physical manifestation of my extreme impatience. Instead of its duration being a few hours or a day or two, it was every time I touched the fan work over the course of two months. It was at times excruciating.

It was somehow effecting a change within me, however, in that by facing into this grating feeling of impatience, not running from it or diverting the feeling by redirecting my attention to something that moved faster, I was actually learning to be truly patient. And as I worked away on my craft in a meditative state with burning sage and the chanting music of the tepee ceremonies, I was also gaining insights into my life: business decisions I had made in haste, life decisions I made out of impatience, conversations I had rushed, and people I had rubbed the wrong way. I was seeing my life in a whole new way and realizing that what I yearned for truly was to slow down, to really hear people, to take in the blessings of life more fully, to enable my intuition to blossom more fully, to have more leisure time, to sometimes be able to just sit with my family and do no particular thing, and ultimately to find a kind of stillness that can only come from forcing oneself into a discipline of long hours of simple tasks, like crafting something to be beautiful, in my case, a fan made of feathers.

Our indigenous people have always known the value of craftwork; they have always leaned toward decorating themselves, their instruments, their tools, their weapons, their clothing, even their horses. I don't think they do this out of vanity; rather, it brings them pleasure simply to labor at making things beautiful. It is just their way.

How then can this simple lesson apply to our daily lives and our business ventures? Let us consider for a moment the rapid and sustained success of the iconic brands in the world such as Harley-Davidson, Coca-Cola, or Nike. Their brands were not developed haphazardly or randomly, but rather through careful development, research, design, and planning, and also through a lot of trial and error, which, again, required even more patience.

Consider the companies that built themselves on an ethic that encompasses something akin to the principle of the four directions, in which all stakeholders are considered. Consider Southwest Airlines, which has not seen a losing year in many decades, even through periods of significant upheaval in their industry such as the post-9/11 declines in air travel. Southwest places a high value on corporate culture, their stock symbol is LUV, and they work with their labor unions as partners. They are considered the airline with a sense of humor, and while there were a number of airline industry bankruptcies following 9/11, Southwest did not make any layoffs or ask for pay givebacks. As a result, their employees continually came up with solutions to ensure good financial performance, as they felt as though they were in partnership with management.[1]

The point is that if we look at the shining examples of successful companies, those that far outperform their peers with consistent enduring results, and we look at how they do it, we'll find that they go deep with their strategy; they look to the long term; they value culture, their employees, their stakeholders, their brand image, and their ethics. In short, they are holistic, which requires time and lots of patience. They are also willing—and this may be the most important distinction—to make short-term sacrifices for long-term benefits simply because they are patient. They can wait for the results they truly want; they can stick out the difficult times with their heads held up, knowing that they have a long-term plan.

In today's tech-oriented world, in which four-month-old software is already considered old, with instantaneous communication, instant gratification, sensory input from myriad forms, huge IPOs from companies that haven't yet turned a profit, and the ubiquitous e-mail culture in which we spend endless hours a day reading and replying, where is there the time to sit back and consider our direction, our focus, our priorities, and the foundation of our businesses and our lives? How have we built our organizations? Have we built them for long-term sustained success or for short-term profitability? Do our businesses reflect our original vision or something better, or perhaps just something different? When do we take time to consider the building blocks, versus scrambling from one fire to the next?

Have we lost our ability to take it slow and careful? If the world around us is continually speeding up, then we tend to go along for the ride and miss out on the experience of building something for the long term. Wall Street expects quick returns and trades billions in value in mere microseconds. In recent years, Wall Street trading firms have been hollowing out high-rise buildings and turning them into server farms just to squeeze milliseconds of speed out of their stock transactions. Recently an 825-mile trench was built between New York and Chicago merely to create a 13.3-millisecond fiber-optic round-trip between the two cities for the purpose of super-fast algorithmic stock trades. Let's just consider this for a minute: blasting out a trench 825 miles long to gain milliseconds in stock trades.[2]

When we respond to a fast-paced world by being fast-paced, we are missing so many signals and indicators that tell us about the health of our businesses. Just as when I slowed down enough to work on the making of a fan I learned so much about my life, through the stillness of mind, things became clearer and my approach to work changed in a significant way. Now when I feel overwhelmed with tasks at hand, instead of scurrying to catch up, I will often step outside to enjoy the sunshine and will always strive to take time to consider the direction and strategy in relation to those tasks immediately in front of me.

There are also times when the current course, while seemingly urgent, is not the best course for the long term, and the best way to proceed is to just ponder the strategy, the context, the system, and the objectives, and ask the question, "Are we on the right course?" I would not have been able to approach business with this level of patience had it not been for the examples and teachings of indigenous culture.

Chapter 10. Intentionality

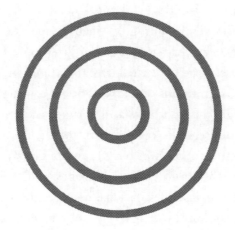

Where there is vision, the people live. They are made rich in the things of the spirit; and then, as the logical next step, they are rich in human life.

—Phil Lane Sr., Yankton Sioux

Many times I have heard newcomers to indigenous ceremonial environments ask what things represent. Each formality seems to spark curiosity about the meaning behind the actions. It is something about the act of ritual itself and the formality of it that is compelling to a good number of people. Indeed, all the elements of indigenous ceremonies hold meaning, and many of the small formalities have stories behind them that, when told, imbue great meaning and value into seemingly inconsequential elements, yet the meanings themselves are not the point of the ceremonies; they are the gateway to intentionality, and through intentionality we are led to the real gift of ceremony.

All the small rituals and formalities, each with their own meanings, collectively represent a process of engagement in physical and mystical acts with clear and highly focused intention. If we engage in the physical acts for the sake of the rituals themselves, then it becomes more about show or simple delight, and the ceremonies become watered down. Indigenous elders, those who reach the state of "walking in beauty," have arrived at a place of wisdom, compassion, and dignity through many years of intentional acts and intentional living.

In chapter 8, "The Four Directions," I spoke of a life changing moment that occurred for me in a ceremony in May 2007. It was when I felt Spirit saying to me, "Now is your time," the time to finally sponsor my own tepee ceremony. What took place over the next few months was a powerful teaching and experience in the power of intentionality.

The morning after the ceremony in which I received this message, I was incapable of doing much of anything, especially the three-and-a-half-hour drive home, as this ceremony had hit me extremely hard. So instead, I stayed with my good friend and brother Whoosh Kaalii in his small off-the-grid home in the Southern California high dessert. At his home, we spoke throughout the day, afternoon, into the evening, and then again the next morning. Or rather I should say I dumped on him about the complete disappointment I was feeling with my life at the time.

I had the trappings of a good life, the visual appearances, the job, professional accomplishments, family, and friends, yet inside I was miserable, and this was the reason for such a difficult ceremony and the clear message of "Now is your time."

Yet what did this message, "Now is your time," mean exactly? I knew in a sense from a deep intuition that the instruction was to sponsor a tepee ceremony, a concept that terrified me to no small degree. It terrified me for so many reasons, one of which was the preparations involved, as there were many; another was the financial costs associated with sponsoring a ceremony of this nature. Yet the greatest fear was that on the day of the ceremony, in the beginning few minutes, I would be asked to bare my soul to a tepee full of my friends, ceremony relations, and perhaps even some newcomers I would not even know. I would be asked to express my intention for the ceremony, the reason and the purpose for which so many people had been gathered, to ask all present, and even a good many not present who would support from afar, to pray for me, for my life, all throughout the night.

It wasn't so much the thought of just having to bare my soul, which is indeed difficult, but also to take a clear stand for my life, to say that on this day I am asking for these feelings and things in my life, this healing and change, and "I am inviting all of you fine people to support me in this request for my life."

Consider this for a moment. When do we take time to publicly proclaim clearly what we want to give and receive from life, or for that matter, just to think deeply about it within ourselves? This is not a thing that is taught or encouraged in our modern culture, as our modern culture teaches us to follow the pack. Yet in present times, there are many people engaged in creating vision boards for this very purpose, and I've heard a number of amazing stories about incredible things happening for people who engage in this process.

And so it is with such a formal ceremonial process; what is required to precede such a day is a great deal of thought, meditation, and counsel on just exactly what that intention is. In my case, and what flowed from my initial hours-long conversation with Whoosh Kaalii, was that what I ultimately wanted was massive life change; I felt my life had become stagnant and unbearable, that trappings of life aside, I didn't like where I lived and worked, the city I lived in, or my marriage. The word *massive* was deliberate and genuine. I knew the saying, "Be careful what you ask for" well enough, yet I was so ready for it, no matter how challenging, difficult, uncomfortable, or even terrifying the changes would be.

For the next two and a half months, I prepared for this ceremony. I traveled to New Mexico, Arizona, the Southern California desert, and the Santa Monica Mountains, as well as around the Los Angeles area, to sit with many of my friends, break bread, tell them my story and what I was asking for, and invite them to my ceremony. For those who came from greater distances, I spoke at length with them over the phone.

There are many natural elements that are required for such a ceremony. The wood for the fire has to be prepared in a specific way—long slender sticks five feet in length, debarked and cleaned. We can't use poplar because it pops too much in the fire. It would be a summertime ceremony, August in the desert, so preferably no hardwoods that would burn too hot; we wanted brightness, not heat.

There were corn husks that we use to roll tobacco smokes in. The husks were requested of a Hopi corn farmer in Arizona, carefully prepared by soaking, forming, trimming to size, pressing, and drying over many days.

There was a lighter stick to be used for the purpose of lighting our smokes. There was a ceremony performed for a cedar tree in Northern Arizona in which we asked permission to take its center pole, made offerings, cut it in a particular way, cleaned the bark right there at the base of the tree, dried it over thirty days, then sanded and shaped it.

There was cedar to be prepared for burning on the coals of the fire throughout the night. Again we made an offering to a cedar tree, took branches, dried them, and painstakingly removed the evergreen from each branch and broke the pieces into a small granular size.

There was the making of gifts for those who contributed to the ceremony and the purchasing of great amounts of food for a grand feast afterward. I purchased Pendleton blankets online and commissioned beadwork. I made sure that everyone who came received some kind of gift and did my best to make sure the gifts reflected the gratitude I held for their contributions to the ceremony and their sacrifices for my life.

In all these preparations and in all these conversations and travels, there was one overarching ever-present element: *intention.*

The intention was a premise for the actions and conversations, but not merely presumed or haphazardly constructed; it was a well-thought-out, carefully articulated request for a different kind of life.

I sought counsel from trusted sources to critique and help refine my request, and each time I told my story and articulated my intention, it became more clear and resolute. As I told my story, I also became more courageous in my resolve and more willing to do whatever was necessary to bring this request to fruition.

How then does intentionality apply to our modern system of business and commerce? I believe in the most important of ways. As the saying goes, "Be careful what you ask for," the same could be said in reverse: "Be careful acting without clarity of intention." In other words, if you act without asking for anything specific or not caring deeply in what you are doing, the result may not be what you really want.

All the great visionary leaders, the movers and shakers as they are known, have always been known for driving a particular vision. We even call them visionaries because we see them as being so special for having such strong vision and the courage and determination to stick to their vision no matter what.

Steve Jobs was a great example of a business leader with a relentless commitment to quality, seemingly at the expense of everything else. More recently, Tony Hsieh, the founder of Zappos.com, who places a great amount of focus on corporate culture and creating an enjoyable working environment, has been able to build a business that passes that enjoyableness, or employee satisfaction, on to his customers in a large and growing measure.[1] There are many examples of such leadership, and they are all similar when it comes to strong visionary leaders. They might fail at times, but always learn and evolve, keep going, and eventually realize something truly amazing.

Strong vision flows from clear intention.

Intention is the foundation of vision, passion, motivation, and creativity. Intention is also unique to each human being, infinitely creative, gloriously expansive and liberating.

We can either accept the construct that the world has given us, or we can form our own personal intention, based on the core of who we are and what we want our lives to be about, and birth that intention into being as our own personal expression of who we are.

There is an old Native American story about two wolves, in which an elder conveys to the children that there is a battle that exists within each of us, a battle between two wolves. One wolf represents love, compassion, trust, and integrity, and the other wolf represents hate, judgment, fear, and dishonesty. Then a child asks the elder, "Which wolf wins?" And the elder answers, "Whichever one you feed."

Positive intention fuels a life of goodness. Negative intention brings about disharmony. Not having a clear intention has the potential to bring about a life of meaninglessness. The choice is yours to make.

There are many layers to intentionality. It is like the layers of an onion; each one peeled off reveals another deeper level. So too with intentionality; the deeper we contemplate and examine our intentions and the more honest we are willing to be with ourselves, deeper levels of our true intent will be revealed. Moreover, we have to be willing to accept whatever truth we find when we dig into our conscious and subconscious intent.

More recently I've found myself having 97 to 98 percent positive intent in most cases, and yet when I have dug deep, I've found inklings of self-centered thought. Prior to my first big sponsored ceremony in the summer of 2007, I would never have been able to look inwardly so honestly and boldly, and I was at times more self-centered than now, particularly in my professional life. Yet as I have progressed on this journey of self-discovery through indigenous culture and religion, I have come to a place of very little self-doubt or self-judgment, which has opened up my ability for deeper levels of self-examination; if I can accept whatever I find within myself without judgment, then there is no fear of what I will find, and therefore, very little resistance to digging deeper.

This is extremely important to the work of intentionality because we are taught by our culture to compare ourselves to others, to hold ourselves up to particular standards, and that how others view us is actually important. If we compare ourselves to others and value the opinions that others have for us, then it creates a condition of continuous self-doubt and self-aggrandizing opinions, or what some people refer to as ego.

If we can set aside our desire for approval from others for just a brief moment, we can come closer to observing our true intentions without self-judgment, and if we can observe our true intentions—all of them— we are moving closer to having clear and powerful intention.

My friends, all I can say is that when we have 100 percent pure, well-thought-out intention, intention that we can own to the core of our being and is authentic to who we are, life becomes amazing and magical. I invite you to dig deep within your thoughts and emotions, and ask yourself continuously what kind of a person and what kind of a leader you want to be. Own what you find and seek to transform your intention to the authentic you.

Chapter 11. Roles of Men and Women

A woman's highest calling is to lead a man to his soul so as to unite him with Source. A man's highest calling is to protect woman so she is free to walk the earth unharmed.

—Cherokee proverb

We must have respect and understanding for women and all female life on this Earth which bears the sacred gift of life.

—Traditional circle of elders, Onondaga

At a gathering of Native Elders we were told that many men of today had lost their ability to look at the Woman in a sacred way. They said we were only looking at Her in a physical sense and had lost the ability to look at Her sacredness. They said the Woman has a powerful position in the Unseen World. She has the special ability to bring forth life. They told us to start showing Her respect and to look upon her in a sacred manner. We must start this today.

—From an elder's meditation, May 15, 2012

When the European settlers first came to North America, they saw that the chiefs were men and therefore made the assumption that the indigenous culture of this continent was patriarchal, like their own. They also saw a clear division of roles in the societies, cooking conducted by the women and hunting by the men, and so they further assumed that a woman's role in Native society was diminutive.

This assumption could not have been further from the truth, as the organization of indigenous culture in a matriarchal framework is nearly consistent throughout the world. In North America, the chiefs were men, but the council of elder women typically appointed the chiefs, and if those chiefs conducted themselves in such a way as to lose the respect of the grandmothers, they would find themselves no longer as chiefs of the people.

In all the ceremonies, there are specific elements that are only conducted by men, and certain other elements only conducted by women. For example, hunting game for a ceremony, drumming, and tending fire are typically reserved to the men, while cooking food for a ceremony is typically reserved to the women. I have found many modern women who are new to these ceremonies to chafe at these practices as they feel the implication is that they are being boxed into roles of diminished importance.

In the modern world in which women are gradually owning more of their power, they have called out their abilities to do anything that men can do as a demonstration of their equality, and yet in our modern culture, there has been and still is to a certain extent, an implication that certain responsibilities should be left to men because they are more capable, and certain other responsibilities should be left to the women because it is beneath the men to do those things. In indigenous culture, the division of roles is all about respecting and honoring the differences between women and men by honoring their God-given strengths. In this context, neither role is considered diminutive.

In every story I've heard about the origins of the ceremonies, they have all come from women—the White Buffalo Calf Woman, who brought the sacred pipe to the Plains Indians; the story of an Apache woman who brought the peyote medicine to help the people of the

Southwest; the story of Arrow Woman, who brought the pipe to the Cherokee people; the story of Sky Woman, who brought the Iroquois people all of their ceremonies; the story of how the sweat-lodge structure is itself representative of the womb of Mother Earth; and so many other stories originating from women.

The women say when the big ceremonies are going to take place and when not; the grandmothers provide the guidance on all the big decisions, and they are the ones with the real power in indigenous culture.

So why, then, would the ceremonial traditions hold as a very important component of protocol that women should prepare the food? In indigenous thinking, the women are the life givers and the nurturers of children, and so as food is a nurturing life-giving thing, it would be best if women prepared the sacred food. Yet to indigenous people, this is not diminutive; rather, they are saying with this tradition that if you want that food to be prepared in the most loving and sacred of ways, who better to do that than the women, who are the most loving and spiritually sacred people?

Why then would the men be expected to hunt the game? It is not that women cannot hunt just as well as men. Yes, men have greater upper-body strength and speed, yet women have agility, stamina, and intelligence. It is because in indigenous culture, men are seen as the physically stronger and less spiritually evolved, so it is better to leave the more aggressive work to the men and the gentle nurturing work to the women.

Many of our modern women would read these words *gentle* and *nurturing* and take that to mean weaker or lesser, and many of our modern men would read the words *stronger* and *aggressive* and take that to mean more capable. Therein lies a sizable portion of the dysfunction of our modern culture, that we associate strength and capabilities with aggression and power. If we turn the paradigm upside down and perceive for just a moment that love and nurturing are about the most powerful attributes a person can express, then the role of fixing food would be seen as a huge honor, not a diminishment of women's place in society, but a holding up high.

The Navajo people have two words for rain, translated to female rain and male rain, with female rain being gentle and male rain being hard. Again, in our modern culture, we would generally take that to mean that female rain is weak or of lesser importance. However, if we look at these references more closely, gentle rain is more enjoyable and better for the land, whereas hard rain tends to bring everything to a stop and send people running for cover. Gentle rain enables the land to absorb the moisture at a slower rate, whereas hard rain can cause flash floods and erosion. Female rain can be seen as beautiful, whereas male rain is more of an obstacle. To the Navajo people, respect for women is woven into the fabric of their language from a mind-set that perceives gentleness as a strength and a good thing.

To indigenous people, a woman's moon time is representative of her role as the keeper of life. To the Native mind-set, life does not occur without woman, and the man's role of providing that spark to the egg is considered of much lesser importance than the woman's, who nurtures her egg into a life. The women are highly sacred because all life comes from them, and when they menstruate each month, they are in a place of higher power, a place in which the essence of their ability to create life is in full bloom.

In our modern patriarchal society, women tend to be looked down upon during their moon time. In indigenous culture a woman on her moon is seen as living in an elevated state of spirituality. In many indigenous traditions, women on their moon are asked to stay away from ceremonies, partially because by the nature of what their cycle represents, they are already in a continuous state of ceremony and therefore do not need to be in ceremony with others; and also because if they participate in ceremonies with others who are not in their heightened state, they could potentially bring harm to those who cannot handle that level of spirituality. It is because women on their moon are so powerful that they are, in essence, too powerful for many to handle.

The important lesson to garner from this is that women on their moon are viewed as so powerful that they are excluded not because of judgment or prejudice, but because of caution that through their elevated state they are too much to handle.

I have also heard it said that men work to keep women in a diminished capacity in society primarily because they are afraid of them, and this follows with indigenous thinking, which holds women as the keepers of life and as being more spiritually evolved than men. Hence the Cherokee proverb "A woman's highest calling is to lead a man to his soul so as to unite him with Source. A man's highest calling is to protect woman so she is free to walk the earth unharmed."

To take an example we can all accept as a truth, we know from study after study that children who do not receive physical contact, love, and nurturing during their early developmental stages have a much higher chance of developing mental illness and learning disabilities. We know this affects their higher learning center and ability to interact with others. In the indigenous mind-set, it is also accepted as a general truth that women are far more naturally adept at providing this kind of nurturing than men, as though it were written into their DNA.

So if we can accept that the role of women as mothers is to ensure that children are raised to be emotionally healthy and understand and possess the ability to give and receive love, then can we not also accept that their role as mothers and nurturers of life is about the single most important role on Earth? And if we can accept that women have the most important role, then wouldn't it also make sense that women have the most powerful abilities, or at a minimum that their abilities are at least equal in importance to those of men? This doesn't mean that men are off the hook related to parenting and nurturing their children; rather, that men have a great deal to learn from women in this way and can follow the woman's example, striving to be more nurturing, and in so doing can allow women to lead him "to his soul."

Again, if we can perceive for a moment that the abilities of an individual to express love and to nurture another unconditionally are more powerful than the ability to act aggressively and be physically powerful, then we have to take a huge pause and reconsider our collective mind-set related to the importance and sacredness of *woman*, or as some in our modern realm would say, the *sacred feminine*.

So how, then, does this apply to the business world? A study published by Catalyst in 2011 showed a distinct contrast in financial performance between Fortune 500 companies with few or no women on their boards, versus those with more women for at least four of the five years that the study examined. One metric in particular showed an outperformance of 84 percent in return on sales (ROS) by companies with three or more women board directors, versus those without women board directors.[1] Another study, by Credit-Suisse, researched nearly 2,400 international companies and concluded that "Stocks with greater gender diversity on their boards ... tend to perform best when markets are falling, deliver higher average ROEs through the cycle, exhibit less volatility in earnings and typically have lower gearing ratios."[2]

In my thinking, this increase in performance is not strictly related to results produced by the women board directors themselves, but also as a result of the more expansive culture that exists within these companies. Cultures that genuinely respect women and their unique talents and attributes are also more likely to genuinely respect and honor differences in the way people think, types of creative processes, different perspectives, cultures, and ethnicities. In other words, more expansive thinking naturally will be more inclusive of women in executive and board-level positions, and the results of more expansive thinking will invite greater innovation and long-term financial success from everyone within an organization.

Another Catalyst study showed that companies with more women in high-level leadership positions are able to expand their talent pool by looking to individuals who do not fit the mold of traditional leadership stereotypes and were also successful in retaining highly talented women based on the awareness of their having better odds at growing within the company.[3]

On a simplistic level, the value and meaning of this indigenous principle of honoring the differences of men and women and respecting their roles is that if women are prevented from advancement to high-level leadership positions, a culture that dissuades creativity and innovation will result, and a culture that dissuades creativity and innovation will in the long term weaken the foundation of an organization.

Corporations and organizations should not necessarily put only women in charge of certain tasks and men in charge of others based on their God-given strengths as this indigenous principle would seemingly imply. The modern working world is very far removed from a lifestyle and work-style that is simple and Earth-based. Even organic food providers have lots of people who sit at desks in front of computers and hold marketing and finance meetings. In other words, our modern business world is such that women and men truly can work effectively, creatively, and dynamically in virtually any role interchangeably. There are certain trade positions like hanging drywall or lumberjack that would be difficult for most, but not all, women to perform, and we don't find there to be an appreciable number of men signing up to be au pairs. The analysis is that roles are fully interchangeable, but any organization that devalues or disenfranchises women is cutting itself short.

On a deeper level, there is something magical that occurs with companies that truly value diversity, and I'm not referring to companies that hire diversity managers to ensure that hiring is balanced, but companies that really get that they will be stronger if they *are* diverse. When companies hire people from all walks of life, with different approaches to creativity, organization, communication, and productivity, and truly celebrate and enjoy that diversity, there is a huge intangible benefit derived that can only be qualified as possessing some special mojo.

Tony Hsieh, founder of Zappos.com and author of *Delivering Happiness: A Path to Profits, Passion, and Purpose*, adopted happiness as a business model and turned a losing venture into a $1.2 billion Internet powerhouse. Many of Zappos's core values align closely with indigenous principles. Number three, "Create fun and a little weirdness" speaks well to the need to respect diversity in organizations.[4] A core value that encourages "a little weirdness" suggests that they are a company that loves people of all kinds. Respect for gender differences and strengths would naturally flow from such a core value. Hiring people of different cultures and ethnicities would not need to be a focus for Zappos because it is already woven into the fabric of their company culture. And their intense and sustained financial success reflects that they indeed have their own special mojo.

Looking again for a moment at the concept of gentleness and

nurturing as being stronger character traits than outward displays of strength and aggression, while that would not necessarily translate to men and women holding different positions in companies based on gender, wouldn't the implication be that we would have to face the fact that the old-school model of competition, a dog-eat-dog world and it's every man out for himself, is a broken and useless model?

There is beauty, intense beauty derived from watching men and women perform in their strengths with intention and dignity. In my first experiences with indigenous culture watching grand entry at the powwows, as the dancers entered the arena in a long procession grouped by gender and style of regalia, I saw the northern traditional men with their huge bustles of eagle feathers dancing the warrior's dance, and the women's traditional dancers in their long buckskin dresses dancing in a most stately and dignified manner. I was in awe—men and women honoring who they are and becoming art in movement.

So much of what we fret and worry about in our lives and in our businesses related to relationships simply fades away when we honor people for who they are, give them a voice, value them, contribute to their happiness, and most importantly, let them shine. In such a state of being, men can feel comfortable showing kindness and nurturing, and women can feel comfortable owning their power and using their voices. Both will be empowered by the other, and as a collective, we will reach new heights.

Chapter 12. Seventh Generation Unborn

Look behind you. See your sons and your daughters. They are your future. Look farther and see your sons' and your daughters' children and their children's children even unto the Seventh Generation. That's the way we were taught. Think about it: you yourself are a Seventh Generation.

—Leon Shenandoah, Onondaga

I see a time of seven generations when all the colors of Mankind will gather under the sacred tree of life, and the whole earth will become one circle again.

—Crazy Horse

Throughout many of these indigenous principles there runs a consistent thread related to connections: connection to Earth, to culture, to the elders, connections between men and women, to the four directions, and even connection to the inanimate. The principle of the seventh generation unborn is an encapsulation of these various ways of looking at connections into one unifying philosophy, that we are all merely part of a whole, not dominant or above, not better than, and certainly not more important than.

The Australian Aboriginals are a good example of an indigenous culture not seeing itself above living systems. The Aborigines do not have words for "left" and "right," as they feel it would be self-centered to refer to directions in relation to one's own perspective. Instead, Aboriginal children from a young age learn to know where north, south, east, and west are, and they have a profound sense of direction that is based on their relationship to Earth, rather than Earth's relationship to them. This reflects a cultural orientation of people living as a part of a system, to which they are a piece of the whole.

The recurring theme of connections leads us to think this way, to set aside our concept of nature and geology existing for the pleasure, comfort, and perpetuation of humanity. Thinking in terms of the seventh generation unborn takes us to an elevated level of community with all living systems, as well as those systems that we might think of as nonliving, like geological systems, which are in fact living in the indigenous mind-set.

In spite of our best efforts to convince humanity otherwise, nature repeatedly shows us that we are not the center of all life and the universe. Copernicus was the first to suggest, in the early sixteenth century, that Earth revolves around the sun, and not the other way around, which was a highly objectionable concept in 1542 when his book was published. Then in the early seventeenth century, when Galileo wrote a book in support of Copernicus's concepts, he was tried, forced to recant, and spent the remainder of his life under house arrest. We resist accepting facts that suggest that we are merely a part of a whole, and not above or superior to living systems, or celestial bodies in the cases of Copernicus and Galileo.

Our observations show us that we live on a planet that revolves around the sun, which revolves around a galaxy, that our solar system is at the outer reaches of our galaxy, that Earth is the third planet from the sun, not the first, that there are many planets orbiting around other stars, and so on. The concept of evolution tells us that we might well have evolved from apes, or at least that we evolved in some way similar to other species, as in Neanderthal man being our genetic predecessor.

We also know that ecologically Earth flourished prior to the rise of the industrial revolution, and we know that if humanity were to go extinct tomorrow, Earth would eventually return to a state of abundant life and healthy ecosystems. Our scientists are telling us that nearly every living ecosystem on Earth today is in a state of decline, and while there have been five major mass extinctions that we know of in Earth's history, the current rate of species decline is far more dramatic than what the fossil records show us about the mass extinctions of the past.[1]

We know that it takes millions of years for geological systems to produce petroleum oil and coal. Basic chemistry tells us that there is a giant amount of carbon sequestered in the form of oil and coal in the ground. We also know that there is a finite amount of oil in the ground, and that burning it in mass quantities changes the atmospheric balance, which leads to other conditions that are presently being heatedly debated.

What is the consistent thread? That we live for ourselves while arguing over the potential long-term effects of our industrial activities, consumption of natural resources, proliferation of chemicals, bioengineered food, and so on.

Living for the seventh generation unborn means that we live each day of our lives with full cognizance that everything we do, every food we eat, every speck of dust we disturb, every piece of trash we leave behind, every natural resource we utilize, as well as every thought we have, the words we use, the kindness or compassion we express, or the selfishness we indulge in all have an effect that can carry through the generations to our great-great-great-great-grandchildren.

Indigenous people look to the seventh generation unborn because considering our lineage well beyond the generations that we will ever have an opportunity to meet requires us to live with such heightened accountability, compassion, and altruism that we are forced to see ourselves as a part of a living ecosystem. Embracing the importance of the lives of the seventh generation unborn places our own lives in the present in a very different context, as we must live and conduct ourselves with more humility and respect for *all* life.

Contained within the philosophy and the principle of living for the seventh generation unborn is also the recognition that the lives we have today are a direct result of the lives of our ancestors seven generations back; that our great-great-great-great-grandparents lived a certain kind of life that led to us. Seeing our lives this way helps us to live in gratitude. It is as though an invisible benefactor bequeathed a huge fortune to us, as to Pip in Dickens's *Great Expectations*. Yet we all have this benefactor, this unseen saint of the past whom we shall never meet and to whom we owe our very lives. In indigenous philosophy, the seeds of our lives were born in the hearts and minds of our ancestors, their ethics, their sacrifices, their hopes and dreams, and not so much—as the Ayn Rand philosophy of rational self-interest suggests—in viewing life's purpose as the pursuit of one's own happiness.

So the principle of the seventh generation unborn requires us to live for those of the future while also acknowledging the seven generations past; to have reverence for our roots and respect for our progeny.

Consider how our present culture tends to place a significant value on our children, the second generation. Some cultures tend to place more attention and value on their grandchildren, the third generation. How would we treat our children and grandchildren if we were thinking about the effects of our actions on their great-great-great-grandchildren? Would we indulge them with pleasures and entertainment to bring them continual happiness? Or would we consider more deeply the character we are helping them to develop that will enable them to become amazing parents to their children, their children's children, and so on? Would we discount them, discredit their ideas, tell them to go away and be quiet, or consider that every word and gesture we utter to them can have a far-reaching effect?

In business, I have seen far-reaching effects of words and actions that ripple through time: my prior unwillingness to apologize for words spoken that were of a selfish nature, which tainted working relationships for years; an executive unwilling to face into controversy for the messiness it can bring, which enabled dysfunction to fester and perpetuate; the fear of middle management to speak out against strategies put forth by upper management that they knew were foolhardy, which enabled a company to steadily flounder and diminish; and self-confidence born of past successes and assumed to mean that all future ideas are sound, which stifled the good ideas of others and destined a company to fade into irrelevance.

I have also seen the relentless pursuit of excellence driven by the passionate vision of a rare few individuals who carry organizations forward with a unified understanding of identity and purpose, which can take decades to tear down by those oriented more around their own self-interest. The vision of those leaders who create organizations based on a deeper, more nuanced definition of success creates lasting organizations, as their vision is not based on themselves, but rather something bigger, something more meaningful, and therefore a vision that employees, customers, investors, and community can more readily get behind and commit themselves to.

My wife, Maria, was raised for the first nine years of her life in Mexico in a poor family, in a home with a dirt floor. Her mother cooked over an open fire, and they grew their own food and raised chickens for eggs and meat. Up until her family emigrated from Mexico when Maria was nine, neither Maria nor her siblings had visited a dentist, and none of them had had a single cavity, as there was no sugar or processed foods in their diet. By the nature of their poverty, they were extremely healthy.

As a little girl, Maria had frequent and severe nosebleeds. At age six or seven, her mother took her to a spiritual healer, who channeled the spirit of a highly revered Mexican indigenous healer known as El Niño Fidencio. The healer channeled, burned frankincense, prayed, and waved her hands over Maria, and her nosebleeds stopped and never returned.

Maria's grandfather, her mother's father, was an Apache medicine person and a practitioner of the sacred tepee ceremonies. Her grandfather had passed away before Maria was born, so she never knew him, yet his teachings carried to her mother in the sense that she had a faith and trust in the indigenous healing ways, which she carried to Maria, and which Maria has carried through her life.

Maria's family was also highly dysfunctional, as her father was an abusive alcoholic, which inflicted deep wounds on Maria's psyche. However, when Maria became a mother, she dedicated herself to breaking the cycle of dysfunction by engaging in a lifelong journey of healing and spiritual evolution. She began living the indigenous principle of the seventh generation unborn.

Maria and I met in our late forties, after I had already spent a good number of years in training and immersion in the indigenous ways and Maria had spent an even longer time in her own spiritual program. As her upbringing, particularly after coming to the United States, was disconnected from her indigenous roots, she had little knowledge of the indigenous traditions. Ironically it was from me, with my largely European ancestry and fourteen years of indigenous training by the time we met, that she was introduced to deeper levels of indigenous traditions.

I wrote about my first experience in a tepee ceremony in chapter 1 and how miserable I was, but it was not just my first ceremony in which I suffered so greatly; it was the better part of my first five years in these ceremonies in which, for the most part, I was a complete mess. All night long in these ceremonies, I would struggle with every fiber of my being to stay awake through the night, to sit up, to be alert and focus on the ceremony, when every cell of my body wanted to lie down and sleep. It took me a long time to develop the kind of strength for these ways that I observed in my indigenous brothers and sisters, to sit fully alert and engaged all night long and to be able to be in service of others and to contribute to the ceremonies.

Maria, on the other hand, had no such struggles. The first time I introduced her to the tepee, she sat all night long with such strength, grace, and presence that it was as though she had been at it for decades. The way we view this is that while there was a single generational break in her lineage from practicing these ceremonies, the prior generations, her grandfather in particular, had carried these traditions through, and her mother, having garnered a small measure of these ways, gave a precious truth to Maria in the form of a lasting healing, so that upon her first visit to the tepee, she felt as though she had finally come home. What carried through the generations to Maria from her Apache heritage was more tangibly realized at the moment she stepped into her first tepee ceremony. You could say she took to it like a fish to water.

We also see that through Maria's strong faith in a higher power and her willingness to do her healing work, she was able to recover from the wounds of an abusive childhood and go on to work with women struggling to find their own faith in higher power and a road to lasting emotional and spiritual health. Maria has an uncommon ability to relate to these women in such a way that comes from a deeply authentic place of knowing the steps that are necessary for women with broken lives to heal, repair, rebuild, and then go on to help others do the same.

Maria grew up in a family one generation broken apart, yet carrying the strength of centuries of connection to indigenous principles and the understandings that come with these principles. Her experiences of time spent with her Apache paternal grandmother, the healing ways of her mother, and her direct experience of miraculous spiritual healing channeled from the spirit of El Niño Fidencio were lessons that held a profound impact for her.

We can all look to our lineage and see the strengths and weaknesses that came from the lives of our ancestors, and if we can see clearly the gifts and challenges that flow from our ancestors, can we not also consider the effects of our own actions, words, and thoughts on the seventh generation unborn, and in having such an awareness, how do we want to conduct ourselves each day, each moment of our lives?

Considering this expansive philosophy of seven generations back and seven generations forward illuminates the need for taking a very long-term view to our business decisions and dealings. The way we treat our employees, customers, suppliers, investors, and community becomes of such heightened importance that we will naturally approach our work in a much more thoughtful and principled way. We will become willing to make short-term sacrifices for long-term gain, while shunning long-term sacrifices for short-term gain. We will develop the discipline to do what is right in the face of chaos or controversy because we will be thinking so far down the road that coping with present-day pain will seem small in comparison to the long-term payoff.

We will also see each relationship, whether it be with individual employees, customers, or suppliers, as being an important piece of a whole. No one will seem irrelevant, and therefore we will cultivate a corporate culture of inclusiveness. When employees prosper within our organizations, we will feel really good about it, not just because of the revenue they bring us, but also because we will know that their enthusiasm for their job is infectious and will carry to others in the organization.

We will build organizations with lasting legacies, that will be celebrated and looked to as the examples to follow, and we will have a whole lot more fun with it than if we were to focus so single-mindedly on how much money we're making now.

Chapter 13. The Oral Tradition

Words hypnotize and deceive everyone at one time or another, but these hypnotic words cannot last long in the hearts of true warriors.

—Barney Bush, Shawnee

The oral tradition is one of the more subtle indigenous principles, yet of no less importance. It is subtle in that in modern civilization, there is a seeming lack of awareness for the effects of various communication styles related to tempo, pause, and listening. For example, character traits such as fast talking, slow talking, or excessive talking are viewed as mere personality traits, not so much in terms of character strengths or defects or good or bad etiquette, but just the nature of the speaker. So we tend not to look more deeply at our own communication styles in relation to our cadence, the pauses we use, or the thoughtfulness of our responses; rather, we focus on avoiding bad character traits, such as interrupting or arguing.

When spending time on North American Native American reservations, one will notice that the pace of communication is very slow and deliberate, and if one is not careful, he or she will talk over people, which typically results in conversations coming to an end. I have found that a great many Native Americans will just not argue, and if one attempts to argue with them, they'll just sit and ponder your words and say nothing, or in some situations they will listen to your point of view and only after a long pause will say something so concise, resolute, and contrary that, at least in my case, I'm left without anything further to say.

Early on in my journey with the Navajo people, in the morning after a ceremony, the time when the people mill around drinking coffee and socializing while a feast is being set up, I was conversing with another non-Indian participant of roughly the same age as myself, and with us was an elder Navajo medicine man. The three of us were just sitting resting after a long night in the tepee. The other non-Indian man started up a conversation in which he was reminiscing about his younger years and experiences with young women. My part in this play was to go along with his conversation because I was treating it like cocktail-party chatter, mindless chitchat about nothing important, being sociable and going with the flow. Then after a few minutes of this, the Navajo elder stood up and in the gentlest of voices said, "One day you will be ashamed of this conversation," and then walked away. And for me, that day did come to pass.

The five nations of the Iroquois, known for their long houses and representative system of government, were also known for long careful deliberation over decisions that were before their people. It has been said that when agreements could not be reached, instead of debating until someone gave in, they would just decide not to decide and no decision would be rendered. So in some respects, there was a motivation to reach agreement in which everyone felt good about a decision and not require that some individuals sacrifice in some decisions for the sake of advancement in another.

Many of these characteristics of indigenous communication flow from their oral tradition of passing down wisdoms through stories from one generation to the next and the ways in which those stories are told.

There is a story about a tribe of Plains people in old times who were caught in a great advancing brush fire on the prairies. These fires could whip up very quickly from high winds in the dry summer months. In this instance, the fire came so fast and furious that all of the people ran as fast as they could to get away from the fire. Then one elder woman shouted to the people to stop running, to turn around and run into the fire, as it was chasing the people faster than they could flee.

Some heeded her wisdom, turned, and ran back into the fire. Others continued to run away from it. It is said that most of those who ran away from the fire perished, that most of those who ran into the fire survived, that the elder woman who called to her people herself perished, and that after this fire, these people came to be known as the Burnt-Thigh People, as most of the survivors burned their thighs from running through the fire.

The meaning derived from this story is that when trouble is chasing us, sometimes the best thing to do is face into it, not to avoid or run away, rather to heed the warrior's call and do the difficult thing for the sake of the greater good. This is just one small example of how wisdoms are handed down through the generations through storytelling, as opposed to parental preaching or the written word.

The way in which these stories are conveyed is of equal importance to the stories themselves. They are told by the elders repeatedly, over and over, until they become engrained into the younger ones, and in this process, the elder is speaking slowly, deliberately, and with emotion, without interruption or distraction, and then after the story is told, its meaning is discussed, or not. There are no quizzes or memorization exercises. The stories are enjoyable, and through their repetition, they gradually become a part of the fundamental makeup of the younger generation.

They are the stories of their culture, their creation stories, stories about the way they dress, the reasons why women do some things and men do others, how men and women are to live in harmony together, how to be a warrior and what that means, hunting stories, stories about where the ceremonies came from, and so on. Through these stories, each generation receives a new link to connect it with a very long chain, representing the continuation of a culture stretching back for thousands of years.

As the younger generations hear these stories and take them on as their own wisdoms and understandings of the world in which they live, they are also learning a style of communication, a way of listening not just to the words, but also to the meanings behind the words. They learn about the power of metaphor, they learn how a slower pace of talking can make communication more enjoyable and engaging for the listener, and they learn the importance of never interrupting. They also learn through these stories how to feel another person's struggles and pain, and they learn the power of perspective and how it can shine new light on situations. It is through these stories that young people can take on wisdoms that would otherwise take many decades of learning through trial and error.

With the cultural value and principle of respecting elders, young people learn good effective communication. Together with a respect for their culture, by learning about it in an enjoyable way, they are given the opportunity to pleasantly choose a kinder, gentler way of being with people, versus being preached to or talked down to and then judged when they fail to follow the edicts of their elders.

In business, there is a carryover effect from our modern-day culture in that without a focus or understanding of the importance of speaking with kindness, thoughtful listening, having an acquired understanding of perspective, and the power of pause, we get into meetings together and all talk over one another. We talk rapidly, and each person jumps in right on the anticipated final word of another, all while the one person with the most insightful thing to say is spending his or her mental focus looking for a window to interject this one thing that can offer a new perspective. The result is that those with the most aggressive communication style or the highest-ranking person in the room is the one who is heard the most, and their ideas may not be the most insightful.

We waste a tremendous amount of time in meetings with this nature of rapid-fire interjection, each person having his or her own perspective, each person fighting to get his or her point across, rather than to just listen quietly and pensively. We also drown out the ideas of the quiet gentle ones because we intimidate them into silence.

As leaders, we need to ask ourselves how well we really listen to those on our teams. I know for myself, there have been many times when I have felt annoyed with suggestions from people on my team, those lower in hierarchy, and then I have had to remind myself to slow down, take a moment, and acknowledge his or her idea, no matter how naive it might be. Even bad ideas can contain kernels of perspective that can add value to a conversation or can serve as an opportunity to mentor a younger executive so he or she can advance in understanding. Even neophytes can contribute game-changing ideas.

Another consistent element of indigenous culture related to communication is the concept of the talking circle. Indigenous cultures do not all do this quite the same way, but they do all sit in circles and talk to work things through. In a circle, no one is above or at the head; all are equal. In talking circles, there is sometimes a talking stick, a feather, or some other mnemonic-like instrument that when held signifies that a person has the floor, and absolutely no one interrupts a person who has the floor. So conversation goes in turns, with each person being given the opportunity to fully express himself or herself without cross-talking or interjection.

The only time we tend to do this in business is at conferences during the Q&A, when we take our turns at the microphone asking questions of the speakers. Some organizations observe good meeting etiquette, in which there is a meeting facilitator who ensures that each agenda item is fully covered and that anyone with something to say on a topic is given the opportunity to express himself or herself before the meeting moves on to the next item.

Meetings take up a lot of time but are so necessary to the work we do. Indeed, the majority of what we do in business is to communicate in one form or another. Therefore, it is imperative that we learn to communicate respectfully, carefully, and deliberately and to listen pensively, patiently, and openly.

The indigenous principle of the oral tradition gives us much to borrow from to enhance our effectiveness, as well as to promote a more enjoyable working culture, in which each person feels valued and creativity is celebrated and in full bloom.

Chapter 14. The Way of Love

In sharing, in loving all and everything, one people naturally found a due portion of the thing they sought, while in fearing, the other found need of conquest.

—Chief Luther Standing Bear, Sioux

Those who live for one another learn that love is the bond of perfect unity.

—Fools Crow, Lakota

The Quiet Elder

In the summer of 2006, I was traveling on the Navajo reservation in Arizona and New Mexico with a friend from Germany and my adopted Navajo brother Daniel. At one point in the trip, we visited a traditional elderly couple who lived very deep into the reservation, many miles from paved roads, electricity, or any signs of modern civilization.

This couple lived in a hogan with a dirt floor. They herded sheep and made woven rugs for their livelihood. Their kitchen was outdoors under an arbor made of vertical timbers sunk in the ground and covered with boards. The husband wore jeans, boots, and a T-shirt. The wife wore the traditional pleated skirt, with lots of turquoise. Their life together was very simple.

In this visit, we were invited into a traditional Navajo sweat ceremony with this elderly man and his grandson. This elderly man hardly spoke a word of English, or perhaps chose not to speak it, and was not very talkative at all really, yet he was warm and gentle in nature.

As we all sat in the sweat together, we really didn't have too much to say to one another, as everything needed to be translated. Daniel and he spoke in Navajo, his grandson spoke a fair amount in English as he was a modern person, and I just mostly listened. The ceremony was hot, but gentle and very enjoyable.

After the ceremony when we had dried off and dressed, I felt it was time to give a gift to this elderly man as I was feeling a certain appreciation for his warmth and humility, yet I was not really sure how he was feeling toward me as we had barely communicated.

One thing I would always do when traveling on the reservation was bring gifts for people, as this is a very Native way of doing things. When you meet new people and make relations with them, there is always an exchange of gifts, and one such as myself, a white man from Los Angeles, who in their eyes was somewhat of a rich man, would not want to find himself in the position of accepting gifts from people who in my eyes were somewhat poor, and not have something to give in return.

I had found people there really appreciated receiving California white sage, as it doesn't grow in Arizona, and so in preparation for my trips, I would trek into the Southern California mountains, pick lots of white sage, clean it, wrap it in small bundles, dry it, and bring it along for gifts.

As I handed a bundle of sage to this elderly man, he took it from me, looked at it, but didn't seem to know what to do with it. I saw confusion on his face. This was highly ironic as the vast majority of non-Indians who participate in indigenous ceremonies widely assume that sage bundles such as the one I had given was universally understood and utilized as sacred medicine. Yet many traditional Navajo people, particularly this traditional elder who had barely set foot off the reservation his entire life, have never seen such a thing.

I then called my brother Daniel over to translate and explain my gift to him. Daniel took the sage bundle and entered into a lengthy description, holding the bundle high up in the air with both hands in a graceful manner, gesturing and speaking for a good couple of minutes.

The Navajo language is highly complex and nuanced and typically takes a lot more words to explain things than in English, as they tend to talk more in story and metaphors than having specific definitions for every concept. To this day, I do not have any idea what Daniel actually said to him, but from what I observed, it was a very detailed description.

When Daniel finished talking, I expected the elderly man to extend his hand to shake with me, as that is the common formality in the exchange of gifts among North American indigenous people. Yet instead, this elderly man grabbed me and pulled me into a warm and firm hug, followed by eye contact and a thank you in Navajo.

In some way, without intending it specifically, I had earned his respect and love. A handshake was not enough; he needed to more demonstratively express his love and respect for me.

A couple of hours later, after more visiting with him and his wife, this elderly man's wife seemed to come alive with smiles and hugs, followed by a group photo, more smiles and hugs, and then sending us on our way, with very little in the way of words exchanged, and yet we had a relationship, and I knew they would never forget me, as I will never forget them.

Daniel

In the summer of 2001, my very first trip to the Navajo reservation, I found myself trapped in a Sun Dance ceremony for eight days. I say trapped because due to a long-standing land dispute between the Hopi and Navajo people, the Hopi Tribal Police blockaded the ceremony as it was being held on disputed land. Since I entered the grounds prior to the blockade going up, I had the choice of leaving and not being able to return, or sticking it out for the entire eight days. I chose the latter.

Daniel was a local, and the locals tended to come to the ceremony grounds each morning and return home in the evening, rather than camping out as those of us coming from hundreds of miles away were doing. As Daniel came to this ceremony expecting to be able to return each evening, he became stuck and chose to stay as well. He had only a pair of cutoff jeans, the T-shirt on his back, the socks on his feet, and a pair of shoes. He worked in the cook shack the entire time, slept on the ground without any bedding, and helped out however he could. He had a stocky frame with skinny legs. His hair was just past shoulder length and quite scraggily. I found myself intrigued by Daniel, as he conducted himself with great humility and moved slowly and deliberately. There was just something about him.

My given task was to work security at the front gate, to help ensure that no one entered the grounds with weapons, alcohol, or cameras, including the Hopi Tribal Police. This was not an easy task given my complete unfamiliarity with the territory and its people, yet it was an important responsibility that fell to me given how many additional helpers who had intended on supporting the ceremony were unable to get through the blockade.

So there I was, a white man in Indian territory at the front lines of a land dispute I knew nothing about, and yet I was there to experience this ceremony, to learn, to grow, and in a sense to find myself.

Twice each day Daniel would bring a pot of hot coffee from the cook shack down to the front gate for two others and me. He would stay for a while; we would talk, drink coffee, and get to know one another. We found commonality in the ceremonies that we practiced. I found that Daniel had been raised by medicine people and trained in the traditional Navajo ways, although he didn't say too much more about that. Mostly we just socialized and enjoyed each other's time.

After the ceremony, we exchanged information, and he took me to his home and showed me where he lived, as out there you can't find places by street signs as there are none. We stayed in touch. He would call me every now and then, and as I was planning another trip out to Arizona and New Mexico the following summer, we decided to travel together. Thus we launched a lifetime friendship, and the following summer Daniel took me as his brother.

This is a distinctly Native concept, to take people as relatives, non-blood-related people, bonded through ceremony and taken into their families. Some tribes even have specific ceremonies for the purpose of adopting people. On a surface level it may seem quaint or sweet to hear people calling each other brother, sister, uncle, nephew, auntie, or niece, yet in the North American indigenous tradition, this is no small thing.

When you are taken or take someone as a relation and proclaim this in ceremony, it is the real deal. You are then family for life, and all the responsibilities and permanence of blood relations are assumed with the same degree of commitment. There is an agreement made that no matter what transgressions, shortcomings, or hardships, you will stick it out together and always love each other. When one spends a number of years in North American indigenous ceremonial circles, one develops a very large extended family, and the beauty in this is indescribable.

There is also a very strong connection to lineage, as this is the way in which indigenous people identify themselves—not in terms of their vocations or interests, but by their family and clan affiliations. When people give a thorough introduction, they will identify themselves with the clan of their mother's grandmother as their principal affiliation, and also list the four clans of each of their grandparents. Listening to their introductions is like hearing stories that describe why a person's life is important, and that places an individual in the world with identity and worth.

So to be taken into their family is a great honor, and yet they do it so readily. They only have to see something in you that they find of beauty and meaning, and they will take you into their families and bless you with their love and warmth for each of your remaining days on Earth. Sure, there are those who may have ulterior motives, yet Natives largely understand that there are certain traditions that you just do not mess around with, and this is one of them.

My road with Daniel has not always been an easy one, as he has struggled for decades with a terrible addiction to alcohol. Yet the depth of his teachings in the traditional ways and the strength of his abilities to move people through prayer and ceremony have continually astonished me. I have seen him at his lowest and worst, and also in states of absolute and complete service in the life of other individuals, giving completely of himself for only a simple request and a gift of tobacco.

The way of love is not so much a direct teaching of indigenous culture as it is a byproduct of their way of life. It is also a principle in that the elders will talk about the need to love our families, our communities, our people, ourselves, and our Earth. Indeed, many of the principles explored in previous chapters indirectly relate to adopting a way of love. If we connect with Earth, then we are loving Earth. If we see that all things are alive, then we are loving all things as sacred. If we are respecting and valuing our elders, then we are also loving them. If we are living for the seventh generation unborn, then we are loving the seventh generation unborn. And if we are communicating as indigenous people do, then we are also loving all those with whom we communicate in that way.

For a full integration of indigenous principles, we cannot hope to understand their way of being if we cannot learn the way of the heart. Taken as a whole, that is what these principles represent, to awaken our feeling, caring, nurturing hearts and adopt the heart as the true driver of who we are, to recognize our intellectual minds as being mere tools by which we conduct business; that we are the carpenter and our intellect is our hammer and saw.

Yet it is the passion of the carpenter that lives to create things out of wood that become useful, productive, and even beautiful. We can in the same way live to create business enterprises that are useful and enriching when we move from the mind to the heart, from analysis to acceptance, from forcefulness to gentleness, and from disconnected discontinuity to four-directional balance of all things.

This word *love* is like a taboo in the business world. We've bought into a mythology that says that how we live our lives is separate and distinct from how we do business; doing business requires us to focus on business fundamentals, meaning bottom-line management. Bottom-line management means we make decisions concerning people and Mother Earth based on numbers on a spreadsheet, even though we know and have been shown numerous examples of companies that transcend industry averages to healthy, consistent, sizable profits, and longevity (Southwest Airlines and Zappos.com mentioned previously, for example) based on an ethic of valuing their people, employees, customers, vendors, and even their communities. Holding people in a place of value and importance represents a caring for their well-being, which is an expression of love.

Practicing the indigenous principles is a process, and like all processes, it requires vigilance, which we will delve into in part 3. Through the daily practice of indigenous principles, our capacity to trust into a state of loving our employees, customers, investors, and vendors will come about naturally, but it also requires us to jump into what may seem like an abyss without a net, as the concept of loving our employees and vendors is antithetical to conventional business thinking. No matter how deeply we move into an understanding of indigenous principles, to integrate *all* these principles will require us to step out of our collective comfort zone and risk behaving and conducting ourselves based on an entirely new paradigm.

The quiet elder didn't contemplate his feelings toward me; he felt, he trusted what he felt, and he expressed his feelings. In the reading of Tony Hsieh's story of growing Zappos.com, there were many occasions in which new levels of success were immediately shared with employees in the form of surprise bonuses. Zappos has a tradition of picking up the tab when dining with vendors, and they go to significant measures to have the checks brought to them first, completely contrary to the conventional thinking that the vendor always pays.[1] In their case, they wish to continually express their gratitude to their vendors. This is trust in the extreme because there is no contract that states they will receive a just reward for their generosity. They are merely expressing their gratitude and trusting that by deepening their relationship with their vendors and employees that the goodwill will be reciprocated. For Zappos.com, strong vendor relationships and a culture of happiness have proven to be the cornerstones of their business model. Doing business with love is the cornerstone to a complete adoption of indigenous principles.

Chapter 15. Integrity

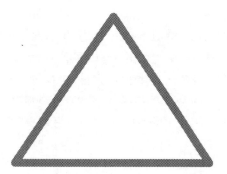

It does not require many words to speak the truth.

       —Chief Joseph, Nez Perce

You must speak straight so that your words may go as sunlight into our hearts.

    —Cochise "Like Ironweed," Chiricahua Apache

Writing about the indigenous principle of integrity is the hardest of all in some respects because there is seemingly so little to say about it as it seems so self-evident and simple. It is as if we could just say, "It is good to be honest and true, and things work better when we conduct ourselves with integrity," and we could end this chapter in one short sentence.

We can expand the conversation a little by pointing out that many indigenous languages do not have words for lying, which reflects a cultural distinction in that not only do many indigenous cultures have a strong ethic of integrity, but the very concept of telling a falsehood is incomprehensible to them.

We can also build on chapter 13 on the principle of the oral tradition, and that by speaking through stories we can convey deeper meanings than what words alone can convey.

I don't think we need to examine the really obvious transgressions of integrity, such as companies like Enron humming along fine, yet wanting more profit and swindling their way to get there, or Bernie Madoff running a massive Ponzi scheme for so many years. We can all agree that examples such as these are well outside of ethical boundaries and do not lead to good long-term results. Perhaps even Madoff would agree to this given where he's presently sitting.

The deeper conversation related to integrity lies in exploring our own internal process and then in looking at the corollaries to the principles of indigenous living.

For myself, I have always placed integrity high on my list of important character traits and have consistently maintained a very high moral discipline in this area. However, almost all of us can point to times in our lives when we have told lies, and while in my own case, those times are extremely few and far between, it becomes very revealing for me to closely examine the reasons and motivations behind my prior transgressions of integrity, and observe what triggered the willingness to lower my standards of self-conduct.

In those few occasions in which I've told a lie, it has always been because I felt I was serving a higher interest, that there was a greater good that would be served by the telling of an untruth. In business, it could be because we think we are protecting a project that we think is valuable from being cut, or an employee whom we value from being laid off, or to close a deal that we think will be good for everyone involved.

It could also be to protect ourselves from political attack or character assassination, particularly when we can perceive the malicious intentions of others, and then say to ourselves that we need to do what we need to do to remedy the situation, that their actions are unkind and unfair and so we need to put a stop to this.

So in the case of being faced with an executive who is making a series of bad decisions, is treating people horribly, and seems to be generally incapable of telling the truth, if we find ourselves working under this person or in some form of partnership or collaboration in which our success is at least partially connected to the conduct of this executive, and we also see that this person has given such an effective snow job to upper management that this person is currently held in very high regard, or perhaps this is the CEO and has full authority to wantonly wreak havoc in the organization, what do we do?

We can resign and go find a more harmonious place to work. We can go to upper management or the board to try and make them aware of things. We can manipulate situations so that this executive fails in such a way as it seems plainly evident that it was his or her fault. We can become a whistle-blower and call him or her out. Or we can just bear it and keep plugging away with the idea that what goes around, comes around.

None of these options seems desirable or necessarily pleasant and certainly not easy.

Another example would be if we see our business failing, the outlook is grim, and we are thinking of all the people who could potentially lose their jobs; then we think of our own financial future, our reputation, the business we built over so many years— "It's our baby, for God's sake." So we devise a scheme to save the company. Perhaps the scheme is legal, but not necessarily ethical. Or perhaps it is both legal and considered ethical, but not necessarily fair to our suppliers or employees or customers or competitors.

I won't try and say what *is* ethical, fair, or with integrity, as each of us needs to ask that question of ourselves and honestly assess our actions and tactics according to our own moral compass. The point is to look very carefully at those really difficult decisions we've made or are being faced with making, and closely examine our motivations, not just the stories we tell ourselves like, "It's for a good cause," "People's jobs depend on it," "Too much is at stake to lose this deal," "This person is dangerous and needs to be curbed," or the more cynical, "What they don't know won't hurt them."

We need to look deeper into our decisions to discover the core underlying motivations. For myself, I have found that whenever I've made a decision that I have felt was not in the highest of integrity or involved the telling of a falsehood, at the core, what drove my rationale for lowering my moral standard was some form of fear.

This is a hard thing for most to grasp, as we don't want to admit to our fears or consider that any of our decisions or actions could be based in fear. Yet anxiety is a form of fear, and anytime we feel anxious toward a decision that needs to be made or a difficult situation that needs to be dealt with, it is a good indicator that fear is at work in us. Anger is another mask of fear. If someone is pushing a direction or an idea that brings up anger in us, then most likely there is a fear at work. Jealousy is another cloak of fear, in that we are afraid that someone else will receive all the credit and we will therefore fade into irrelevance.

The constant drive for profit is all too often misrepresented as a need to focus on objectives, when it may really be about the value of one's stock options or annual bonus. Yes, there are financial considerations related to a company's credit worthiness that flow from its current stock valuation, but what if we could forget our own financial status for just a moment to look at our decisions without the fear of what shareholders and Wall Street analysts will say? Perhaps we would arrive at entirely different conclusions. Isn't fear of negative outcomes from analysts and shareholders clouding our judgment and driving us to sacrifice long-term benefits for short-term gain?

Then there are perhaps more subtle, little decisions that we may make on a more frequent basis that are not truly in integrity, but that have become a habit, like exaggerating the attributes of a product, or avoiding telling an employee the truth about something because we don't want to upset him or her, or fudging numbers on a spreadsheet to tell a story the way we want it told, or making up stories to delay a project, or string along a deal, or bring about anxiety in others to gain leverage in the deal close.

In most cases I have found, there are still fears motivating the transgressions of integrity. We must ask ourselves, therefore, do we want our decisions and actions driven by fear, or motivated by passion, creativity, and vision?

Some might say at this point, "Yeah, but ..." and then go on to list the reasons why certain decisions need to be made, certain words exchanged or not exchanged, and the stories we use to justify the actions. You might be thinking, "Yes, this sounds great, but it is very idealistic, and we have to run a business first and foremost to make a profit," and "We have to protect the bottom line," and "We can't let this secret get out because ..." and "We have to protect this product line because ..." and so on.

The response that flows from indigenous culture is that we exist as a part of a sacred circle of life, the four directions; that all things are inherently connected, that everything is alive; that every action sets things in motion for the next seven generations unborn; that we strive to be patient and take a long-term approach to our work; that we look deeply to our core motivations, our intentionality; that the words that we use are not themselves as important as the meaning behind them, as in the oral tradition; and that we think of the highest good in all our actions, the way of love. Many, if not all, of the indigenous principles relate in some way or another to the need for living our lives with very high ethical standards.

It goes without saying that the need for integrity is self-evident, yet the lessons from our indigenous brothers and sisters is that it is not important to be honest so that people will think of us as good people, or that our company is good, or so that we can think of ourselves as being good people or running or working for a good company; the need for integrity is so highly important because it is necessary in order to be right with all that we are connected with ... which is everything.

Speaking untruths, whether perceived or not by the recipient, sets in motion a disease of the mind, mostly in us, but also in others. Recipients of untruths may not perceive the deception, yet will not feel right about things. They may not be able to put their finger on what it is, but will feel that something is off. This will affect their working relationships with people. It will affect how they will feel about their work, their company, and their coworkers and will carry into everything they do.

When we speak untruths, even if we think it is to protect someone or for a greater good, it creates a condition in us that hinders our ability to hold ourselves in high self-respect and dignity, and when we are unable to hold ourselves in a place of high self-respect and dignity, then it is difficult to treat others with high respect and dignity. So our actions carry forward, potentially for seven generations.

There are also times when telling the truth will genuinely hurt people, and we may feel that not telling them or telling an untruth is necessary in order to protect them. The importance of integrity in these instances is the hardest to convey, yet it is no less important than in situations in which not speaking has an obvious detrimental effect. Again I would say that in indigenous thinking, we must speak truthfully because it is necessary in order to be right with *all* things, which does not mean that we speak callously or without understanding and compassion. But it *does* mean that we must speak that which needs to be spoken.

Jack Welch famously wrote and spoke about the need to tell underperforming employees where they are falling short and even letting them go when needed, and that such an action can actually help them progress on a personal level.[1] I can admit to failing in this regard in that for certain employees for whom I felt great affection, it became extremely difficult for me to consider letting them go when situations warranted it, or even to just more directly address their shortfalls. Integrity for me in these instances has been challenging in the past.

I have also personally suffered under a management too meek to confront conflicts that were of minor significance. Due to a complete unwillingness to face into the controversy, those conflicts smoldered and festered over a period of time and affected long-term outcomes. Then when we were faced with a greater conflict, there was a tendency to overreact based on a pent-up frustration with the lingering smaller conflicts. The way of the indigenous is to continuously strive for balance and harmony, which means that we must speak the truth even when it's uncomfortable or may hurt the feelings of some.

The method I have utilized to discover the necessary course or response in these situations is to closely follow the teaching of intentionality, to check my motives on the deepest level and ask what the purpose of sharing these words is. Then I ask myself what is in the highest and best good. Is it to speak up or keep it to myself? If I ask myself what is in the highest and longest-term benefit while checking my motives, then I can more readily come to a place of clarity.

The other tool I use is to consider *how* I can use my words. Taking from the principle of the oral tradition, I can use stories and analogies. Taking from the principle of the way of love, I can speak with kindness. Taking from the principle of the warrior spirit, to be covered in chapter 18, I can gather my courage to do what is right regardless of how difficult it may be.

Even in the face of controversy, if I follow these principles and do what is right, it may seem messy or difficult in the short term, but I always find that in the long term, things will be much better than I could have imagined them being, and I will simply feel good about it. It might be that it will take six months to a year to see the long-term benefit, but the long-term benefit always reveals itself at some point in time and gives me cause for gratitude for these understandings and for having followed the indigenous principles.

In thinking of the need for honest communication, I'm reminded of the story I wrote about in chapter 13, "The Oral Tradition," of the Navajo elder who stood up and said, "One day you will be ashamed of this conversation" and then walked away. I am also reminded of too many instances in which someone directly lied to me, and while at the time I was not completely aware of their deception, I still felt something off, something not quite right.

The more we move into a fuller appreciation for indigenous principles and practice them daily, the more we will sharpen our intuition and *feel* when things are off in this way. In addition, by coming to know what it *feels* like to be on the receiving end of transgressions of integrity, we will be powerfully motivated to strengthen our own level of integrity. As the principle of the four directions teaches us, we are all connected and to stay in balance and harmony, to be right with all things, we must strengthen our integrity.

Chapter 16. The Spirit World

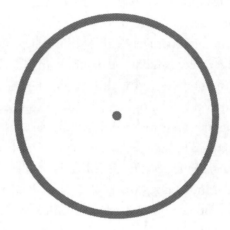

One of the things the old people taught me about the spirits was to never have a doubt.

—Wallace Black Elk, Lakota

While this author has endeavored to present the most vital of indigenous principles applicable to the modern business world and to do so in as secular a way as possible, this chapter may be hard for some to accept. And so I would only ask that the reader keep an open mind and consider that there could be good and beautiful corollaries with religions that merely use different language to speak of essentially the same thing, such as angels, spirits, guides, deities, and so on.

This principle is really more than a principle to indigenous people; it is a knowing and an intrinsic part of their daily living. Indeed, this is likely the most important of all indigenous concepts as it speaks to the original source of their wisdoms. Few indigenous cultures have developed written languages specifically because they have not felt the need to record information that flows freely to them whenever needed on any topic from the most trusted source of wisdom—the spirit world.

The first time I heard Spirit speak to me in a way in which it was utterly undeniable was in the summer of 2005 in a sweat-lodge ceremony with my good brother Daniel, at his family's place in Hard Rock, Arizona. It was a men's lodge ceremony, with just a few of us, Daniel running the ceremony, a nephew carrying the rocks, two older brothers, and myself.

The sweat-lodge ceremony is one in which a lodge is built by bending freshly cut willow branches or tree saplings to create a dome shape. Their ends are sunk in the ground at the perimeter, and the rounded shape is kept in form by lashing the saplings together with twine in a particular shape. Lodges can vary in size, but typically are just large enough for about ten people to squeeze in and sit very closely to one another. Lodges are typically no more than five feet high.

The lodge is then covered with lots of blankets to keep the heat in and the light out. In the old days, when game was plentiful, they were covered with skins. In the Navajo style, there is a door opening that faces the east. The fire that is in line with the east, an altar in between the fire and the lodge, the door to the lodge, and a small pit in the center of the lodge in which hot rocks are placed are all in a perfect line from east to west.

Large rocks are heated in the fire over the course of two hours until they become glowing red. Once the rocks are hot, everyone enters the lodge, and the rocks are brought in one by one in four groupings for four rounds or four doors. The person running the ceremony pours water over the hot rocks, which produces steam. To begin each round, a door is brought down to contain the steam and create an environment of total darkness for the purpose of non-distraction. Songs are sung, prayers are spoken, and words are exchanged.

At that point in my life, I had been doing a lot of work with the ceremonies and my personal spiritual healing and development. I also had a great deal of stress in my life on every level, and was carrying what felt like a huge load continually weighing me down.

And so there I was, sitting in the west side of this lodge, round after round, praying for my life and my relations. The rounds would last from twenty to thirty minutes, after which the door would be opened, letting light in and steam out for a period of rest before the next round would begin.

Just before the third round began, as the new supply of hot rocks were brought in, one rock in particular tumbled over the pile to lie right near me, as I was sitting in the back of the lodge. As these rocks were volcanic, they had rough surfaces. The way in which this rock glowed red as it fell into position and faced me displayed dozens of little smiley faces staring directly at me. These were like perfect little faces similar to the 1970s' yellow-shirt variety.

And so this gave me cause to allow myself to feel a little happier, to just sit reflecting on the message of this rock. As the door was closed and more water was poured, most of the water missed this rock, as it was on the far side of the pit from where Daniel was pouring, so it continued to glow smiley faces at me throughout this round.

When the door was opened signaling the end of the third round, there was still plenty of heat emanating from this rock. Again, more rocks were brought in and the door was closed, and again since this rock was at the far side of the pit from Daniel, it remained unmoved and uncovered from the third round. As the fourth round began with the forthcoming curtain of darkness, what had been dozens of little smiley faces morphed into one large smiley face encompassing the entire rock—one large effigy of serenity continuing to face me.

It was at this time that I heard the voice of Spirit in a most unmistakable way, with one simple message, "Be happy." It was as if Bobby McFerrin just channeled through this rock, and while this may seem too simple to be real, the full meaning of this took months for me to fully integrate, that while there was much work yet to be done in my life, the simple choice to "be happy" reverberated within me. I was offered a simple choice for a new way to look at my life—to be grateful.

As the fourth and final door was called signaling the end of the ceremony, as the light spilled in and the remaining water in the pit continued to simmer as the rocks released their final heat, I reached out and laid my hand on this rock of many faces, this newfound friend, and the emotion that came over me at this time was indescribable; it was a moment of pure joy.

This was just a simple message from Spirit that for me was profound and long-lasting; our indigenous friends somehow seem to possess a much more direct level of connection with Spirit. It's as if it is genetic or hereditary in that what seems to come so naturally to the indigenous typically takes many years of training for those whom I have known in these circles that come from European ancestry such as myself. Countless times I have been told things by indigenous medicine people that seem to ring rich with truth, that flow directly from their conduit to the mystical dimension of Spirit.

What is the message in this for those of us born of a modern society that bases wisdom on proven facts, scientific method, trial and error, and analytical thought? I think perhaps the message is that we should not be too overconfident in what we think we know when it becomes evident that we live in an unexplainable world, unexplainable by the constructs of science and analysis, unexplainable by our minds alone. I think Albert Einstein had it right when he said, "The only real valuable thing is intuition."[1]

While our scientific community continues to work toward the goal of sending a manned mission to Mars, we still haven't visited the bottom of the Mariana Trench, and we continue to pull bizarre creatures from the depths of the ocean. We still argue over the effects of industrial activities on CO_2 levels as ocean levels and temperatures rise. There are indigenous head-hunting tribes that have yet to be touched by the modern world, their culture therefore remaining without understanding or comprehension by modern society. Quantum physics, arguably the most complex of our scientific disciplines, only yields more questions than answers, despite the greatest of minds dedicating their lives to its study.

Yet in a remote community on the Navajo reservation in Arizona, there are medicine people performing ceremonies that engage the spirit world, providing messages of wisdom to those who seek answers, messages that are so keenly perfect in their timing and delivery as to possess life-changing potential for the recipients from a simple invocation brought on by the utilization of natural elements: wood, air, fire, rocks, water, and steam.

These indigenous relations of ours know something the modern world does not easily comprehend. There is a reason that many indigenous cultures around the world perform a very similar ritual with the utilization of hot steam in a small enclosed environment together with song and prayer. They know these things because Spirit spoke it to them, and because they had the humility to follow the teachings, to be willing to work hard and sacrifice for these ceremonies, and then to receive all that flows from them.

I apologize to the reader if this message seems too religious or mystical to be applicable to the business world, yet as I said at the outset, what I have learned is that all that does not work about the business world is really what is incongruent with tribal cultures with a strong connection to Mother Earth, and all that works beautifully in the business world is actually very compatible.

If we can study the atom for centuries and know less than when we started, can we not accept that the chaos, confusion, dysfunction, unpredictability, self-centeredness, discontinuity, and greed in which we all too often find ourselves enmeshed in the business world flows from our disconnection from the great mystery, the world of Spirit? The moment we think we know something about how our businesses truly operate, are we not cutting ourselves off from further learning, creativity, and discovery of truth?

The message from our indigenous relations related to their connection to the spirit world is very mystical and also very humbling. There is no university degree in the world that will gain a student the same kind of access to the spirit world that these medicine people have. There are no numbers of books read that will gain entry for the reader. I couldn't even begin to provide a twenty-point list of things to do to reach their level of access because the list would be radically different for each person. The point is that what we do not know is so incredibly vaster than what we do know, and if our physicists can't even agree on downward or upward causation as being the root of causality, surely we are looking in the wrong direction for our insights.

As the immortal Albert Einstein said himself, "Everyone who is seriously involved in the pursuit of science becomes convinced that a spirit is manifest in the laws of the Universe—a spirit vastly superior to that of man, and one in the face of which we with our modest powers must feel humble. In this way the pursuit of science leads to a religious feeling of a special sort, which is indeed quite different from the religiosity of someone more naive." It is interesting to note that Einstein was a stated agnostic and that in this quote he does not use the word *God*, but rather speaks of a *spirit* that exists within the laws of the universe.[2] This philosophy is completely congruent with the indigenous perception that sees the hand of Spirit in all of nature.

The principle of the spirit world is truly vast and precisely consistent from one end of the globe to the other in the indigenous mind-set. It relates to all levels of their society. It is the starting point and the ending point for their understandings. Direct connection with this universe of knowledge and guidance is what anoints the medicine person with the right to perform ceremonies and healings. It is the guiding voice in their ceremonies, interrelationships, planting cycles, direction for hunts, ways to resolve conflict, and so much more.

Having a strong sense of intuition, a subtle guiding voice that compels us toward a given end, is like reaching first base, whereas reaching home plate would represent the domain of a fully ordained medicine person. Unfortunately our modern society does not give us the training to advance beyond first base, and reaching first base alone can be challenging when our lives are filled with myriad forms of media, super-fast electronic communications, so many mind-altering substances, both legal and illicit, all serving to drown out the voice of Spirit. In particular, when we work at a frenzied pace for long hours ending in collapse at the end of each day, only to rise in the morning and begin the hustle again, we are unable to slow down enough to reach a place of patience and stillness, and cannot possibly connect with the spirit world in such a state of mind.

Taking on a daily practice of meditation is a good starting point for enhancing one's intuition and over time coming to a place of more direct contact with the spirit world. Spending quality time in nature, without the iPod, the cold beer or soda, sleeping on the ground, taking long hikes alone, finding secluded spots, sitting and meditating with nature for half a day or more can be incredibly healing and rejuvenating, and is also just the sort of thing that can draw us closer to our own personal connection with Spirit.

There is a tendency in some of our major organized religions to promulgate the notion that connection to God is achieved through the authority of specifically ordained individuals, yet the indigenous philosophy is that each person can and should seek his or her own personal connection to Spirit, to receive his or her own guidance and direction without the filter of other humans serving in the role of intermediary. There are times when medicine people will convey messages from Spirit to those in need, but such messages are never presented as though their word is final, only to consider the words and do with them what the receiver wishes.

There are also charlatans in our modern world of so many followers of the indigenous ceremonies, both of Native ancestry and non-Indian, who purport to hold a direct connection to Spirit so that they may espouse great wisdoms to the people. Fortunately for those who truly understand the indigenous philosophy of Spirit, they are easy to spot, for as soon as they start telling a person what to do, we know they are not speaking from Spirit. If they put themselves out there with great authority, then they are suspect.

We also have a trend of seeking out psychics and asking them to tell us our fortune, when all we really need to do is develop our own personal connection to Spirit to receive our own guidance. The true psychics have the ability to validate our own sense of self and our lives, while the charlatan psychics can mislead and manipulate our thinking. The only way to tell the difference is through developing our own personal connection to Spirit.

Until we reach that level of full two-way communication with Spirit, we must accept that what we do not know is far greater than what we do know, and in such a light we must approach the spirit world with respect and humility. We do not go to the home of the leading theoretical physicist for a dinner party and proceed to tell him or her all about quantum physics. We also do not visit the realm of Spirit and then tell all our friends and associates that we now know this or that. The relationship we develop is *personal,* and the guidance we receive is our own.

The important thing to know is to take time developing this relationship. Our sense will begin with a strengthening of our intuition, which is enough for now. Then over time, we can go further; we can communicate, we can ask questions and receive answers to our most puzzling conundrums and challenging quagmires. The relationship develops as we learn to discern the difference between our egoic mind, the chatterbox in between our ears, and the voice of Spirit. This can take many years for most people to develop. Many of our indigenous relations, however, are born with this ability, or can access it with relative ease once they awaken their spiritual walk in life. I believe this ability is written into their DNA. Not all possess this ability, but a sizable number of them do.

If we get ahead of ourselves and start to equate our inner voice with that of Spirit when we haven't yet taken the time to develop and determine our life's intention and cultivate the ability to reach a state of stillness, then we may be deceiving ourselves. We may have just found a new way to rationalize our decisions by crediting them to our guidance from Spirit.

Opening and developing our heart space, our ability to connect with people and nature, with our hearts and not our minds, is part of the process of developing our ability to discern between egoic thought and guidance from Spirit. This is a process that takes lots of time, perhaps a lifetime of effort for most. It has been said that the longest journey is the road from the head to the heart. This journey can also be looked upon as the road from disconnected mind-thought to connection with Spirit, and integration of analysis with intuition. These indigenous principles offer for us a practice, a road map, a journey exactly this distance of mind to heart, from the intellectual to the intuitive, and from the coldly justified to the compassionate warrior.

For me it has been a long road to evolve from the ability to hear two simple words, "Be happy," in a powerful sweat-lodge ceremony conducted by a medicine person in the presence of traditional Navajo people deep in their reservation, to a place where I can readily access guidance and teachings, and more importantly, serve as a conduit for Spirit to work through me in the effort of bringing about peace and balance in the world. I am not yet to home base, merely progressing forward one step at a time, continually checking myself, stepping back, asking again to receive clarity, saying thank you, then stepping forward with gentleness, and at times caution born of the desire to stay in tune with Spirit and not to overpower with my own personal will.

This is about the most rewarding principle my indigenous relatives have been able to convey to me, as it represents the building of a lifelong relationship with a mostly benevolent universe of spirit beings, always at my side and ready to assist, always accepting and loving me in a space of continuous healing and growth. The peace and joy that come from this connection are indescribable. The peace that flows from approaching my work with an inner knowing that flows from this connection is profound. Connection to Spirit affords us the ability to conduct our business and our lives with ease and grace, to shed conflict and drama, to more powerfully develop strategy, intention, and vision, to convey them with clarity, and to be the kind of leader we have always dreamed of being.

Part III: Integration

We believe that the teachings of our ancestors will light our way through an uncertain future.

—from Grandmothers Counsel the World

Chapter 17. Organizational Change Starts with Ourselves

These are our times and our responsibilities. Every human being has a sacred duty to protect the welfare of our Mother Earth, from whom all life comes. In order to do this, we must recognize the enemy—the one within us. We must begin with ourselves ...

—Leon Shenandoah, Onondaga

At this point in our exploration of the principles for indigenous living, considering the purpose of these principles, their meanings, and even their beauty, we have come to the most important part of this book: What do we do with them?

The answer, in short, is both easy and hard. Or perhaps stated differently, it is simple but not easy. It is easy because the wisdoms that flow from the integration of these principles bring about a much easier way of living, working, and experiencing life. The hard part is that it requires us to change in a very fundamental way, letting go of patterns of thought brought about by modern culture and the values contained within it.

The need for us to personally change on a core level lies at the foundation of paradigm change, and unwillingness to change is foundational to why so many attempts at it fail or are only partially successful. We cannot ask an organization to change if we as its leaders are not willing to do so ourselves.

At the risk of sounding overly simplistic, we know that we cannot be the kind of leaders who say, "Do as I say, not as I do," yet on a particular level, just below conscious thought, there is a tendency to think that being in a place of high leadership, we are somehow immune to the need to live by the same rules of conduct as those lower on the proverbial food chain. There is a tendency for many in leadership to feel entitled to live by a different set of rules, and our ability to check ourselves in this process will determine how successful we will be in bringing about personal change that leads to organizational change.

Even if we have been changing ourselves for the past forty years and think we are really good at it, when we take over a company that requires great change, we have to remain willing to learn and change every day, recognizing change as a constant. This willingness on our part to consider our need for change and actually do it will be seen and felt by others and will permeate through our organizations. People will be more open to change when they see it in their leaders.

Having said this, let us consider a different track for a moment. We run the company, department, or division. We alone set the rules. The team needs to follow the rules that we set. If not, we'll build a new team; we will find other people willing to do it our way.

Okay, ask yourself honestly, how many times have you seen this track actually work? If you can find people willing to do things the way you want without question, how long will your company remain successful? I think we know the answer to this question, as it has been written about extensively and is almost self-evident. Those who still adhere to this top-down do-as-I-say style of management are simply not paying attention to all the great thought leaders on the topic of management and leadership.

What we really want are people who think for themselves dynamically, creatively, and expansively, take ownership for their work, take accountability for their mistakes, learn from their mistakes, and then continue to innovate. We do not want people following a prescribed doctrine; rather, we want them following an unwritten code of conduct that says, "I believe in this company, its brand, its image, its mission, and its product or service. I'm going to do what it takes to be successful. I'm going to do my work well, with integrity and passion."

The simple answer is that it starts at the top and works its way down; it starts with an organization's leadership. Whatever the values are that we aspire to engender in our organization, we have to first *be* those values ourselves. If we want people with integrity, we have to *be* people of integrity. If we want cooperative leadership, we have to *be* cooperative leaders.

Being the person we want to see in our organization on every level can very well be the hardest thing we have ever had to do in life, but I can say with absolute conviction that it is entirely worth the ride.

When we talk about changing organizations by changing ourselves, what do we really mean by "changing ourselves"? In this context, I am very clearly not talking about structural changes, although those can definitely result. I'm not referring to policy changes, and yet they too can result. I'm not talking about new strategies, or creating or eliminating departments or divisions; rather, I'm talking about the kind of change that is more elusive, and yet far more powerful—our own paradigm for living life as creative visionary leaders.

The twelve indigenous principles we have just explored represent a powerful set of values and states of *being*, which taken as a whole, bring about paradigm change on a profound scale. Integration of these principles will bring about long-term prosperity while doing the work we truly love and find fulfilling; we will have enriching relationships with our employees, colleagues, clients, vendors, and constituents; we will have a balanced lifestyle; we will effortlessly follow a much higher moral code and feel really good about it; we will continually seek greater levels of balance with nature; and our organizations will move toward an overall state of balance.

Each of these principles requires introspection and self-examination, a willingness on our part to consider our failings, or as some would say, our character defects, as well as our true strengths. Part of the reason paradigm change fails much of the time is because we read great books on the topic by great authors, we hire great consultants, trainers, and coaches who come into our organizations and put on amazing dazzling workshops, and then when we've finished reading that last great book or shook hands and sent the trainer on his or her way, we feel perhaps invigorated by all the amazing wisdom, observations, insights, and conversations—and then what?

Do we actually know what it takes to implement all those great wisdoms wafting through our minds following an intense workshop with a notable thought leader or trainer? Perhaps we can intellectually grasp all that's been said or read, but how well are we at putting those wisdoms to work? It's not that we will grasp all of it or none of it. We *will* grasp and implement something, and the more we explore, the more we will learn and implement, but will it be enough to really shift the direction of our organizations in a positive direction, and what is it exactly that slows or inhibits our change and growth?

The world of business and commerce has taken a largely linear analytical approach to change, and bases many of its decisions on marketing studies, demographics, and financials. Statistics have become the god of decision making in many organizations, and in many instances, enables highly intelligent choices. Yet when we are endeavoring to change our core paradigm for living life as creative visionary leaders by reducing the process to intellectually grasping, analyzing, and processing, then we will not reach our goal. It is not that intellectually grasping, analyzing, and processing is not important; it is that it's not enough.

Change is a twofold process of learning, analyzing, and processing on the one hand, and on the other hand, exploring our emotional responses, delving into them, embracing them, sitting with them, and then allowing them to settle and eventually dissipate. If we keep the process in our head, a linear intellectual process of analysis, our change will be slow and very limited. Conversely, if we are only focusing on our emotional responses and seeking to improve our emotional health, our change will eventually stagnate as well.

The wisdom that flows from our indigenous friends related to change is this: the great mystery of the magical, mystical, beautiful indigenous traditions is their ceremonies.

Indigenous people have been conducting ceremonies with carefully constructed and observed formalities and protocols, handed down through the generations, granted from the spirit world, treated with great respect and reverence, going to great lengths and physical sacrifice to perform for the combined purposes of communing with the spirit world and receiving the teachings of the elders, and in so doing, elevate a person's emotional responses to his or her connection with Spirit and the teachings of the elders. Taken together and understood in their relationship to one another, the participant can achieve limitless change.

It is really that simple.

However, I'm not prescribing that everyone adopt the ceremonial traditions of indigenous people, as most will likely already have a tradition of their own, and others who perhaps do not, may not feel so inclined toward indigenous traditions. The purpose of this book is not religious conversion, but rather organizational transformation in a secular, yet meaningful and perhaps philosophical, fashion.

The prescription for change, therefore, is to take from indigenous wisdoms all that we can related to unblocking our resistance to change, as the process of change is what flows from all of their principles when practiced with earnestness. Spending time in nature on nature's terms has the potential to elevate our emotions; considering that all things are alive, seeing oneself as a part of a larger system, respecting elders, respecting the genders, being patient and intentional, elevating our integrity, communicating in a heartfelt way, coming from love, and reaching to the spirit world all have the ability to bring about elevated emotional responses, particularly when we do this work in relation to how we wish to see our careers, our businesses, our families, and our lives.

When we deeply consider each of these principles while allowing our emotions to flow, we are well on our way toward significant paradigm shift for living life as creative visionary leaders. When we deny or stifle our emotional responses, then we are limiting our growth and expecting, or perhaps hoping, that by our intellectual understanding of these principles the changes will just happen.

Those in our organizations who are already attuned to the kinds of changes implied by the indigenous principles will likely get it, connect with the principles, and effect changes in their work, but most will not. Most will hear your words and consider them as more wonderful-sounding platitudes for positive change and go right back to their business-as-usual desks and continue on.

The tipping point to significant organizational change starts with our own willingness to change, and that willingness requires our willingness to feel. I've heard it said by a number of executives that we need to avoid the touchy–feely. Oddly enough, I've heard this from women executives existing in mostly male-dominated industries and working really hard to compete on terms set by those in dominance. The lesson from the roles of men and women (chapter 11) is that those attributes unique to the feminine makeup, such as gentleness and compassion, are actually strengths, while power and aggression are seen more as weaknesses. Compassion is one strength in particular that brings about great emotional responses, and those emotions should not be suppressed or frowned upon.

Yet we resist our emotions, more so in business than in any other place it seems. It's as though there is an unwritten rule that says that "It's just business," and we aren't supposed to emotionalize anything. Perhaps that's the problem: we've separated business from life, such as in the example of the carpenter serving the hammer and saw, versus the hammer and saw serving the carpenter.

It's convenient at times to perpetuate the myth that emotions have no place in business, as it makes it possible for us not to have to look at our own emotions, not to have to feel and embrace our emotions, because many of them are uncomfortable. Which is exactly the point of the difficult nature of indigenous ceremonies being so physically challenging: they help us to develop great inner strength, and if we are observant and pay attention to the metaphors and examples of ceremony, we will learn that everything in them relates to aspects of our daily lives.

So the lesson for organizational change is to feel, and to feel all those things that are uncomfortable to feel, because as we do so, we will elevate ourselves to new levels of understandings and an enhanced ability to conduct ourselves more precisely according to our highest ideals and values. In other words, through consistent sacrifice, we'll learn to walk our talk, and by walking our talk we'll set the example and create the space for others to do the same.

Chapter 18. The Warrior Spirit

It is not through the great skill of the hunter himself that success is achieved, but through the hunter's awareness of his place in Creation and his relationship to all things.

—Thomas Yellowtail, Crow

The concept of the warrior is one that transcends many cultures and geographies and yet is predominant in older cultures far more than it is embraced in our modern world. It is often misunderstood to imply a person who is employed in the vocation of physical violence, whether seeming justified or not. Indeed, my Mac widget defines it as "A brave or experienced soldier or fighter."

This definition could not be more inaccurate as the concept is understood in indigenous cultures. The warrior spirit, in the indigenous sense, is exemplified by people, men or women, who have vowed their lives to the betterment of their family, community, and nation, collectively their people, and they will act and make decisions for that greater good regardless of how hard it may be or the consequences as they pertain to the warrior himself or herself.

Back in the day of the Indian wars in this country—the physical Indian wars that is, and I say that because the war against Indian people has not ended in the United States, only it is no longer violent in the way that it used to be—the concept of the warrior referred to those who would go into battle willing to die if necessary in order to protect their lands and their people. They would make a conscious decision to do so and openly proclaim their intention to their community; they would at times vow no retreat.

What made them a warrior was not their willingness to go into battle and how they fought; rather, it was the vow to live their life for the protection and betterment of their people at all costs. Thus, the concept of the warrior is expansive and can apply to all aspects of our lives and our world.

In relation to our businesses, and more importantly, our willingness to change, this concept bears significant importance. Indeed, the concept and practice of the warrior spirit is yet another important indigenous principle and is being presented in this section of this book given its high importance related to the implementation of the principles.

There is a common tendency experienced almost universally that when things are bad, the chips are down, and our pain level is therefore high, we then become willing to do seemingly anything to make the changes necessary to bring about positive change. It is at this time that people take on the attributes of the warrior and will perform herculean and courageous acts to remedy problems and face shortcomings.

Yet with most people, there is also a tendency that once things start getting a little better and our emotional pain level subsides somewhat, we back off on the process of internal change or changes that can be painful. *When the pain of change is greater than the pain of not changing, we tend to stop changing.*

What is different about the warrior is his or her willingness to suffer pain, whether physical, emotional, or situational, for the greater good, the longer-term good, the good of our people, our families, communities, and companies even when the pain is greater than the pain that comes with standing still. Or as the Chinese proverb conveys, "Be not afraid of going slowly; be only afraid of standing still."

Unfortunately, we have constructed a very elaborate culture in our modern day that revolves around ease, luxury, and instant gratification such that we have largely lost the ability or desire to suffer for a greater good. When we live lives of so much comfort and ease, personal sacrifice becomes too difficult to bear. It is like a muscle that we haven't used for a very long time that has weakened and atrophied.

If we look at the marketing that we are constantly barraged with from the perspective of the cultural values conveyed, we quickly see what the marketing professionals have determined to be the core desires that, when triggered, will convey positive feelings associated with their products and ultimately result in buying decisions. Touting electronic gadgetry without necessarily showing its applicability to our daily lives, comfort, luxury, instantaneousness, horsepower, and of course, the broad appeal of using sexual innuendo to push products show how we are most powerfully and effectively motivated. Humor is also a strong motivator, which can be a very positive thing, yet marketing through humor does not necessarily work for all brands.

These emotional responses suggest that we are essentially vulnerable to the desires that bring us pleasure and a release from pain without any care for broader or longer-term outcomes. Moreover, this has become not just commonplace or culturally acceptable, but intrinsic to our way of thinking—to always be striving for greater levels of comfort and ease, yet more through a superficial process of product and service acquisition that brings about an exchange of release from pain for monetary compensation.

Therefore this process leads us to place an overemphasis on the acquisition of money, as we see the attainment of it as the universal elixir to cure all ills. If we can learn anything from our indigenous brothers and sisters, it is that they live their lives from an entirely different set of values. The principle of the four directions tells us that everything is connected, the principle of connection to Earth tells us that our very lives depend on the health of our natural environment, the principle of the spirit world helps us to touch the vast unknown and never become too confident in what we know as what we don't know is so much greater, and the principle of intentionality shows us that our lives work best when we act with carefully thought-out intention.

Acting with carefully thought-out intention means we are thinking more broadly, with a long-term perspective. Even if our decisions are entirely self-centered, we can still make significant improvements in our lives and our work by extending our thought process beyond immediate gratification. Even more powerfully, we can dramatically change outcomes by looking for the connections between serving others and our own success. In either case, we are required to be willing to experience some degree of pain, perhaps more than what we are typically accustomed to, for the sake of positive change. We are required to behave like warriors, willing to do what it takes for the greater good regardless of what it requires of ourselves personally.

Let us look at some examples.

How many times have we either observed in others, or perhaps even in ourselves, the tendency to work projects in a particular direction that brings about maximum exposure for the project leader or executive in charge, versus what is truly best for the company as a whole, sacrificing long-term gain for the company so the leader can look good?

How many times have we experienced lingering conflicts between people that fester and become a cancer in an organization simply because the one executive who is in the right position to bring the conflict out and address it head-on is too adverse to conflict?

How many times have we let valuable employees sink into low morale because we have been unwilling to really hear them, empathize with them, genuinely consider their grievances, or consider that there could be any validity to their concerns?

How many times have we cut staffing levels when we know we are cutting into the real heart of an organization, simply to show short-term gains in stock prices?

How many times have we made decisions based on the need for ideas to come from ourselves, or seen others do this, when we know there is another direction that is stronger, bolder, and more innovative, simply because of an insecurity about a person's worth in an organization, a fear that by ideas flowing from this person, his or her worth in the organization is somehow validated?

How many times have we curtailed innovation because it's scary, or observed others doing this?

How many times have we made decisions based solely on financial considerations, or directly experienced the wreckage of such decisions?

Can we not see that decisions made entirely on financial considerations are essentially decisions born of fear and shortsighted self-interest, decisions in which the hammer and saw rule the carpenter? Rather, would it not be better to consider the type of hammer to use, the size and type of the saw, and to consider them both in relation to the nature of the piece of wood the carpenter is working with, the skill and experience level of the carpenter, and the long-term use of the thing being built?

Fear is all-pervasive in the business world and in our modern culture in general. There is no magic pill to take to overcome this condition of constriction and myopic thinking, yet there is a road to follow as laid before us by indigenous people, one that brings about a stronger, inner will driven by a connection to things of meaning and true importance for humanity as a whole. This inner-will becomes strengthened over time from consistent effort. With courage drawn from the cultivation of a warrior spirit, we become increasingly willing to face things that previously we would not have thought possible.

The principle of the warrior spirit is foundational to all twelve of the indigenous principles we have explored thus far, as discovery of the principles and the values contained within them will be only skin-deep if we do not employ the warrior spirit in our efforts to understand them. When we look on the surface of these principles, the self-evident portions of them, it is as if we are peeling the first layer of the onion. If we accept our surface understanding and skip to the next principle, we will be leaving the core of the onion unexplored. It is through the consistent practice of the warrior spirit that we become increasingly stronger and more able to keep peeling the layers, going deeper, and discovering far more profound levels of values contained within the principles. It is when we reach the core of the onion that we transcend the ordinary and become true innovators and agents for positive change.

Chapter 19. Creating Purpose

> Peace comes within the souls of men when they realize their relationship, their oneness, with the universe and all its powers, and when they realize that at the center of the Universe dwells Wakan-Tanka, and that this center is really everywhere, it is within each of us.
>
> —Black Elk (Hehaka Sapa), Oglala Sioux

The example we see of tribal living in cultures with a strong connection to Earth is that they all share certain noble character traits, such as respect for elders, respect for women, fearlessness, integrity, and humility. Above all, they also value purpose. They do not follow lives of purpose for the sake of serving themselves; rather, they see themselves as interconnected and interdependent—just as every business that exists in the world is interconnected and interdependent, so too is every family, every community, and every ecosystem.

There are many threads that weave themselves throughout the indigenous principles, with just a few that are overarching; these threads are interconnected and somewhat sequential. For example, we began our exploration of indigenous principles with the starting point of connection to Earth, and from there we moved to everything is alive, the elders, and then the four directions. We could actually stop right there, delve deeply into these four principles, and as a result bring about a powerful shift in our thinking and leadership paradigm.

With these four principles, we would know that we live in a system, that we are a piece of a whole, that we do not have dominion over anyone or anything, that life flows harmoniously when we observe our interconnectedness to all things, and that we can learn these wisdoms from the elders so that when we become elders ourselves, we can pass these wisdoms on and ensure that future generations can enjoy the same, if not a better, quality of life as we have.

The connecting thread is that we are all connected, to everyone and everything, including past and future generations.

The eight indigenous principles explored in chapters nine through sixteen help us to understand that, in addition to ensuring the prosperity and health of future generations, there are deeper meanings and a richer existence that we can access through the practice of these principles in our daily lives. It is my sincere hope that if the reader can take only one thing from this book, it would be to understand that when we drive ourselves single-mindedly toward the attainment of profits and wealth, we are living a very small and meaningless life, and by the nature of our leadership and the effects of our leadership on the lives of others, we are restricting a great many others from discovering lives of deeper meaning and purpose, at least in their working lives.

In the thirteenth indigenous principle explored, the warrior spirit, we looked at the need or value of doing what is necessary or right, regardless of how difficult it may be, and with this final principle, we can bridge the gap between shallowness and meaning. When we preach the mantra of profit and financial objectives, we are in essence giving into our fears, as we are giving into concerns about what will happen if we stop focusing on the money—What will Wall Street say? What will our investors say? What will my peers think of me if I'm not doing well financially? What will my life look like if I make less money? And so on.

On the other hand, when we commit ourselves to the warrior spirit and doing right by people, we might do things like dedicate a portion of profits to a particular charity that is of concern to us or dedicate support to our local community; we might encourage valuable employees to discover their passion in life and even help them achieve it, even if it means they will leave our employ; we might seek to develop a discernible career path for each and every one of our employees; we might readily acknowledge our mistakes to employees, investors, or customers; we might be willing to take time and gradually repair and rebuild business units that are underperforming versus selling them off, shutting them down, or shipping them overseas; we might commit ourselves to local sourcing, even though acquisition costs are higher; we might do many things that we would otherwise not do were we to be driven single-mindedly by profits.

And yet, all these selfless things have consistently proven to be effective tools to strengthen a company's financial performance, as demonstrated in *Firms of Endearment* by Sisodia, Wolfe, and Sheth.[1] The warrior's path is to take our focus off ourselves and place it onto others, and to trust that our own well-being will just be taken care of, mysteriously, mystically, or coincidentally, however you choose to look at it.

When we lead our organizations in such a way, we will have powerfully shifted our paradigm into a place of purpose, and when we move our leadership paradigm to a place of purpose, we will inspire and motivate our teams in such a way as never before imagined. No motivational speaker, no rah-rah-cheerleading trainer will ever accomplish what we can accomplish simply, easily, and effectively by just taking the focus off ourselves, and broadening it, expanding it, and giving life to the principle of *us* as a collective.

This does not mean that every company must exist for some higher moral purpose like Ben & Jerry's with their Rainforest Crunch ice cream flavor and community ethic, or Patagonia and their environmental ethic, or Zappos.com and their family culture, or so many other companies doing amazing things. Purpose can be derived for the local tire shop simply by the nature of the leader believing in and respecting his employees and being dedicated to doing quality work for his customers. Purpose can be created in the small manufacturer who makes brackets for the auto industry by being dedicated to sustainable manufacturing practices, creating flexible work schedules for parents of small children, having a child-care center in the plant, sharing profits with employees, and just caring about each of the people associated with the company.

We all need toilet-bowl scrubbers, windshield wipers, cleaning supplies, soap, plumbers, electricians, and carpenters. Producing these items and providing these services can be just a means to the end of making money, or they can be purpose-driven by infusing them with the higher purpose of caring about people and the environment and providing high-quality products and services with integrity.

When employees see that their company truly walks the talk of higher ethics and values, they will get behind their company. They will work harder for a company that values them in return, and they will be encouraged to do the right thing regardless of it being easy or hard, simply because they have seen their leadership setting the example of the warrior spirit.

Creating purpose is such a simple thing, and so joyous and fun. The hard part is departing from the fear of the what-ifs to the wisdom of "I'm doing this because it feels right."

A number of years ago in my work of producing large-scale festivals, I used to work with a sign company that produced a large quantity of signs and banners for a sizable public festival I was managing. This company was and is the largest sign-manufacturing and installation company in Southern California, if not the West Coast. At first I resisted working with them as they were not the least expensive vendor on the market, yet once I did, I found their capabilities to be unparalleled and so continued to deepen my working relationship with them.

In the process of working with this company, I came to work more closely at times with Howard, the president of the company. Howard founded his company in 1972, built it from scratch, had become very financially successful, and yet continued to work, not just in the company, but engaged in the day-to-day process of producing signs. He had turned over much of the management to his son and yet stayed involved in the manufacturing. Why? Because he loves making signs.

To many, manufacturing signs might seem like a very unexciting thing to do. Let's face it, how many young people answer the question of what they want to do when they grow up with, "I want to make signs." Yet it is a necessary profession, like the vast majority of mundane services and products. In the case of this particular sign company, the owner and founder has a particular passion for producing signs. He loves the technology, the machinery, the people who work for him, and he loves a challenge.

In the business of producing outdoor festivals with a business model that relies on large cash sponsorships, there are many instances in which it becomes necessary to develop signs and banners in difficult locations with odd sizes and tricky installations, and in those odd and tricky situations, I would typically call Howard directly and share my challenge with him. In every instance he would get excited about the challenge of coming up with a solution and would say, "Let me work on this and get back to you." He would always quickly work up a solution and get back to me, and his solutions would consistently work.

From my perspective, I loved the opportunity to work with someone who loved his work so much, as there is a certain integrity that flows from a person doing what he or she feels passionate about, no matter what it is. Make no mistake, Howard went into business for himself because he wanted *the good life*. He wanted, and has since achieved, financial success, but he also loves his employees and treats them really well, evidenced by the fact that the average length of employment at his company is twenty years. He openly expresses his appreciation for the work they do and creates the kind of work environment that fosters enough of a happiness index that his people don't want to leave.

At the end of the day, they are producing signs, what many would consider to be mundane, and their services are not the least expensive, yet their work is very high quality, their customer service is impeccable, and they are very consistent, and so year after year, they continue to prosper. They are purpose-driven in that they have a culture that believes in pride in workmanship and taking care of people, employees, and customers. They are not saving the rainforests—in fact, they use a lot of vinyl and chemicals in their manufacturing process—but they have enough of a meaningful purpose that they have stayed strong while most of their competitors have gone out of business.

One could suggest that there are other factors for their success, and I'm sure there are, yet culture is so critical to the long-term success of a company. If employees are happy, they will infect their customers with their happiness, they will feel more greatly motivated to go the extra mile for their customers, and they will feel personally invested *in* their company because they feel personally valued *by* their company.

I have a good friend and colleague named Jon, who runs a small construction company in North Carolina. He began his career as a tradesman at age seventeen and started his first construction company at age twenty-one. For a number of years, he directed a nonprofit construction company in New Jersey, with the objectives of providing jobs and quality low-income housing. After moving to North Carolina in 2001, he started another construction company, building custom homes and custom additions and renovations.

Jon greatly enjoys the relationships he develops with his clients, approaching each project with the goal of making every effort to understand what his clients want, and then advising them on the best ways of accomplishing their goals with the resources available to them. Jon misses not being able to build affordable housing for low-income families, yet still feels fulfilled in that he is providing quality jobs to his staff, one of which is his son.

Jon lives a simple life; he is not much into high tech and he doesn't aspire to build a giant construction empire, yet values are highly important to him. I have come to know him through my nonprofit work and have watched him work tirelessly and with great sincerity in the effort of helping others achieve a better life. Jon would most prefer to build affordable housing for low-income families, yet loves working with his clients and most importantly the livelihood that he provides for his team. The respect he gives his people is very high, and the result is a stable company.

He is very clear about why he is in business and what his purpose is. By working with integrity and quality craftsmanship, and generating stable employment for his team, he maintains a thriving business, always busy, always with projects in motion. Jon also does not market his company; he does not even have a website and relies completely on word of mouth to find new clients. His purpose drives his culture, and his culture drives his business; quality work, meaningful relationships, and fair terms and treatment mean continued business, and by Jon's standards, a good life.

I have a close personal friend who is a plumber and also a Cherokee elder who shared a story with me of how he passed his contractor's exam with flying colors. While many can find the exams to be challenging, he described how he breezed through it once he came to the realization that plumbing, at its core, is a system that works on gravity and pressure. He conveyed that if you understand the relationship of pressure and gravity and that it is one complete living system, it is scalable and transferable to any situation, no matter how large or complex. Then he related plumbing to life itself, as an interdependent system.

So my plumber/philosopher friend doesn't just connect pipes, elbows, and fixtures; he creates systems that work as a whole. He finds his work fascinating and challenging, and approaches it with a deep confidence born of the understanding of the science of plumbing serving as a metaphor for harmonious living. To quote my plumber/philosopher friend, who goes by the name of Terry,

> A plumbing system is a machine that works like a perpetual machine that is in perpetual motion. It's like an engine that feeds and breathes and exhales. Plumbing is way beyond just a connection of pipes and fixtures; it's an actual living-breathing machine, an entity. You can actually create a plumbing system that requires no energy that operates based on the *breath* of the machine. If I take that breath away from it, it will not work, it takes the breath to make it work, which is what gives it its life.
>
> We are a creation, and we are creating things that we don't fully understand. We keep bringing in the knowledge, but all the knowledge in the world will not give us the understanding. It needs no gas, no fuel to run, just the air that feeds the system. It's a perpetual system. It runs a hundred years without a lick of fuel being given to it. It will definitely outlive us.
>
> The reason I was able to pass that test wasn't just from the knowledge. It was when a lightbulb went off, and I had a complete understanding. There was no test I couldn't pass. I could build a whole city of plumbing. Once it clicks like a lightbulb, "Oh, I've got it," then you are the master of what you're holding. I think sometimes knowledge prevents us from having the understanding.

Prior to hearing Terry's words, I never gave plumbing much of a thought, other than the inconveniences that come from stopped-up drains or leaky pipes, yet I feel a certain respect for someone who feels so deeply about a trade and the work of simply being in service. He's found his own meaning and purpose in the art of plumbing, just as the owner of the sign company, the owner of a local construction company, the manufacturer of everyday widgets, and so on.

It is a wonderful joyous thing to work in a profession like environmental law working to save the spawning grounds of the gray whale, or in the health profession saving lives, or as a fireman, minister, counselor, or sustainability consultant. It can be equally as joyous to work in a profession that is not so obviously altruistic, because at the core, all professions are engaged in the act of helping people, and the how of how we do it flows from our purpose and is also what determines our culture and our leadership paradigm.

Even a company making janitorial supplies such as urinal screens can find purpose, as several companies have by making them out of recycled plastic. The founder of California-based Hot Dog on a Stick, a restaurant chain with a simple menu and quirky uniforms, found purpose by deeply valuing his employees and passing 100 percent of the ownership of the company to its ESOP (employee stock-ownership plan) upon his passing in 1991.[2] Today this company continues to thrive.

And so here is the simple answer to transforming business: we evolve our purpose, define it, live it day to day, walk and talk it even when it is hard, sticky, difficult, scary, or we are just plain unsure of what to do; and as we live our purpose every day of our lives, others will follow. Some will sign on with us, others will move away from us, and in the end we will have a team, a tribe, a community of peers, of people we love and respect, who have our backs because we have theirs and who love our vision because it's theirs too. We will learn each day from the people we work with, and they in turn will learn from us.

The teaching we receive from the indigenous principles is that in order for this to work, we must work at it, that there are many steps to defining a purpose that is one that people will resonate with and get behind in a powerful way. We cannot simply *will* our way to culture change. There is no consultant, trainer, or coach who can come in and do what they do and expect our culture to just change. We can have all the coaching sessions, seminars, and workshops in the world, but if we as leaders are not willing to do the hard, sticky, difficult work of delving deeply into our own personal process, we will only change the window dressing without addressing the core conditions that led us to where we are today.

The end result of doing this work is profoundly satisfying and fulfilling, as it brings us into a fuller understanding of who we are and what our purpose is in life. This work empowers us to achieve things that we never before thought possible. We will discover a calm confidence, relinquish the need to control others, release regrets and resentments, learn to appreciate diversity of thought, celebrate creativity and innovation, and accept and embrace setbacks as opportunities to learn, all as fringe benefits to the greater gift of healthy, thriving, successful organizations.

Chapter 20. Creating Core Values

Grandfather says ... you must not hurt anybody or do harm to anyone. You must not fight. Do right always. It will give you satisfaction in life.

—Wovoka, Paiute

Every business has a set of core values, whether they are stated or implied, and those core values are what shape the culture of a business. It's not even so much about the example that senior management sets, and yet their example is highly important; it is that the values that permeate through each individual decision, policy, and strategy are felt on a visceral level by every employee. Vendors and customers also feel these values, as when they interact with employees, they too feel them on a visceral level.

On the surface we assume the purpose of business and commerce is to make money, yet if profit were the *only* reason, we would have an overabundance of people going into high-yield businesses such as pizza parlors, donut shops, or selling illicit drugs.

One could say that people start the kinds of businesses that they are personally familiar with or have expertise in, while their underlying motivation is profit, which could be true for the most part. Yet what attracts people to particular types of businesses in the first place? Even the serial entrepreneurs are people who find interest in the various products and services they are launching, and their excitement might come from creating new things and new businesses, not necessarily from running them for the long haul. In their case, the value system may simply be creating new and interesting things.

If a person decides to start a broom-manufacturing plant, he or she might care very little for brooms but perhaps sees an opportunity based on a broom shortage, or a physical space in an area that is economically depressed with a city greatly motivated to attract new manufacturing. Perhaps the purpose is to make money, but he or she may also like the idea of manufacturing useful things, or the idea of employing people who badly need work, or maybe creating a stable business that he or she can hand down to his or her children.

Perhaps there are industrialists who believe in the concept of mass automation, a controllable workforce, cost controls, and profit maximization, and employees are just numbers to them. Perhaps their only motivation is profit, but if we dig deeper, we will always find more purpose than just making money. Whether their purpose is altruistic or not, there is always more under the surface. In this type of example, ego gratification can play a sizable role in a person's motivation.

There is another motivation that is both powerful and subtle that is a driving force in our modern-day business culture. It is a belief system that is an acceptance of the notion that driving profits and constant growth is our ultimate and number one goal. This single-minded belief system in profit and growth is so widely accepted that it tends to drown out a deeper approach that brings greater meaning and purpose to the work we do.

When a value system is this pervasive, it becomes cultural, meaning that when we widely accept a given value system to be self-evident and appropriate, we are then motivated by a subtle yet powerful desire to fit in with the rest of society and to be accepted. So in this context, the motivation is to fit in.

Much of what we've been examining with these thirteen indigenous principles is a set of values that collectively frame a different kind of culture, a culture that functions based on a different kind of belief system, one that says that living for the whole is more desirable than living for the self, that everyone is unique and therefore important, that how we make our living is not separate from how we live our lives or engage with our families and communities—in sum, that how we live and work is all one and the same.

The action of *creating core values* is really a misnomer, as what we are really doing is *identifying core values*, the core values that we already have, and then revising them as needed so they are inclusive, respectful of all life, and to some degree or another serve a greater good, so that those who sign on to our vision, whether as investors, customers, team members, or vendors, find something meaningful in it for them.

It is through enhanced meaning that customers and employees become more than just customers and employees; they become advocates and partners. Advocates and partners will do our marketing for us and help ensure that our businesses live strong well into the future.

The potential for investors to become partners and advocates based on enhanced meaning also exists, as the investor climate has been gradually shifting in a direction toward social and environmental investing. The concept of the angel investor is one in which an individual, or group of individuals, invest in projects that they get excited about. The concept of an institutional investor is one in which risk mitigation and return on investment are, for the most part, the sole motivations.

The angel-investor approach to funding is much more consistent with the value system implied by indigenous culture in that the angel-investor personally believes in the founding person or team, the idea, the concept, and the product or service, and he or she will continue to help with coaching and advocacy and serve as an ongoing cheerleader. Defining and then enhancing our core values will increase our chances of attracting angel investors who are like-minded and therefore willing to become personally invested in our mission and vision.

Sincerity is of paramount importance when identifying core values. As an example, Enron's motto was "Respect, Integrity, Communication and Excellence."[1] This might have worked for them for a spell, yet this level of disingenuousness is felt on a visceral level, even if unknown in the conscious understanding that we have toward a particular company. The effect of Enron's deception was therefore short-lived and inevitably backfired.

The collective wisdom of the indigenous principles is that step-by-step, principle-by-principle, we learn that there is a greater purpose to our existence and that to separate this knowing from our business efforts will lead us down the road to businesses that flounder and sputter, or that profit wildly while burning through employees or contaminating our ecosystem, or profit mildly while corporate culture remains rooted in drama and dysfunction.

By employing the indigenous principles and practicing them on a daily basis, we will effect a personal internal shift in our value system, which we will be able to powerfully reflect outward in our organizations and teams. It is through this powerful shift in value systems that culture, that steadfast seemingly unchangeable and unadaptable construct that directs behaviors in organizations, will shift as well.

It is through the formation of stated and demonstrated value systems that organizations will feel compelled to change. It is like observing a flock of birds flying in perfect formation, somehow sensing when the flock will change directions and then all at once hundreds of birds will instantaneously shift direction in perfect unison.

By inculcating a value system that brings meaning and purpose, corporate culture will shift on its own. Not that it will necessarily be effortless, in that there are some people who will have to leave and others to be found to join the team who are more in alignment with the new value system. Some long-established systems will have to be abolished, thus throwing the jobs of some into obsolescence. Yet with a new culture based on values that engender meaning and purpose, our organizations will be revitalized, new projects and systems will come about, and innovation will flourish.

It is the denial of these indigenous wisdoms that led the industrialists of the late nineteenth and early twentieth centuries to believe that people could be turned into automatons, semi-programmable robots designed to work at predictable rates of speed, performing repetitive tasks for a predetermined sum of money, and be fulfilled. It is true that we can devise, and have devised, an economic system that turns people into automatons, but they are not fulfilled in their work, nor do they feel a sense of higher purpose.

Two of our great thought leaders of present day, Gary Hamel and Seth Godin, preach the mantra of the death of the industrial era, the death of mass, and the emergence of a corporate culture that brings happiness, creativity, and value. Another thought leader and friend, Meridith Elliot Powell, author of *Winning in the Trust and Value Economy,* wrote, "We are living in economic times when transparency, authenticity and truly doing the right thing not only pay off but are the only ways to truly thrive."[2]

People are hungering for deeper meaning in life and in work, and they are showing us this by how they respond to products and services and the kinds of work environments they gravitate toward or away from. People in need will take a job to earn a paycheck when it's not what they really want to do because we are taught from an early age that this is what we *must* do. Yet taking a job, or giving someone a job that is unfulfilling, does not bring about an organization of people committed to a common purpose, and without common purpose, we as leaders are beholden to the ebbs and flows of cultural tides, mediocrity, and dysfunction.

Therefore, the goal is to first define our values and then endeavor to enhance them in such a way as to bring meaning and purpose to those invested or engaged in our companies; those values need to be authentic reflections to the core of our being of who we truly are.

As Socrates once said, "The unexamined life is not worth living." This process requires deep introspection and self-examination, and this book and its exploration of these thirteen indigenous principles provides a framework and a guide to examining age-old wisdoms that have empowered indigenous people to live harmoniously since long before the age of recorded history. True, there are many exceptions, but even within warring tribes, there were elders and wisdoms that when their communities chose to follow, led them to peace and prosperity.

I know this to be true because of my years of immersion in this culture and all of the trips I have taken to the reservations, ceremonies attended, relations made, and teachings received. Even with the dysfunctions of alcoholism, drug abuse, child neglect and abuse, severe poverty, and diabetes, I have met elders and genuine medicine people who are incredibly humble human beings, who possess ancient teachings and wisdoms. Even in the face of so much estrangement from their traditional way of living and surviving, there are still pockets of wisdom and beauty that I have had the privilege to touch and experience.

Taking time to be in nature in a very connected way, contemplating our place in the world as a part of a larger living system, considering the gift of womanhood and her nurturing intuitive strengths, really listening to elders and engaging their wisdom, being patient, being intentional, being loving, cultivating a connection to Spirit, bringing forth the warrior within—all of these things bring about self-discovery. Through these principles, self-discovery will elegantly bring us to a place of deeper meaning and purpose from which our core values will flow and which others will feel compelled to be a part of.

The key takeaway is to engage in deep self-examination, to explore the values we already have, then to assess those values in relation to the values inherent in indigenous principles, and then to expand upon our core values. We do not necessarily need to transform our businesses into saintly institutions driven to save the world. It can be as simple as providing interesting jobs with an opportunity for career advancement, functioning with high integrity and respect, and employing sustainable practices. Whatever our core values are, they must be genuine, and they must offer something of meaning.

"Too simple," you might be thinking. Yes, simple, but not easy. That is why embracing the warrior spirit is so central to achieving success in the process of culture shift. Examining one's personal motivations on a deep level is not something we are taught in business school, nor in our society at large. Our culture revolves around instant gratification, constant sensory input, myriad forms of entertainment, and the ever-increasing drive toward status and recognition. These cultural attributes are inconsistent with indigenous culture and block us from the ability to get still and quiet and to contemplate our purpose on a deeper level.

We must block out the voice of culture, the chatterbox in our minds that dictates what we should or shouldn't be thinking, doing, or achieving. The principle of the warrior spirit teaches us to do what is right regardless of how easy or hard it may be. If we look within and discover a deeper purpose that we would like to have in our lives, the next step is to live that deeper purpose and to begin that life through the formation of a stated and demonstrated value system that engenders deeper meaning and purpose for those in our circle, our businesses, our groups, our families, and our tribes.

The late Ray Anderson, founder and chairman of Interface Inc., one of the world's largest carpet manufacturers, decided in the 1990s that just being successful in the manufacture and sales of carpet was not enough. He realized that environmentally, carpet manufacturing was disastrous, and so he set out to transform his industry to a more sustainable one. He was not 100 percent successful in achieving this, yet he accomplished a great deal in mitigation of the detrimental effects of his industry and paved the way for other manufacturers to seek a different path, and in so doing created a much higher purpose for his company, which resulted in strong financial performance.

In the example of the West Coast sign manufacturer discussed in the previous chapter, Howard created and maintained an admirable culture that fostered longevity, hard work, and diligence, which has led to long-term sustained financial success. Yet he could go further and become a leader in transforming the sign industry into one that is friendlier to Earth; he could become to the sign industry what Ray Anderson was to the carpet industry.

For Interface, it's possible that there could have been room for a deepening of their purpose as well. We can always deepen our purpose. We can always go further, create more meaning, and become more of a trendsetter and a guiding light for others to follow. We don't have to try too hard, though, to deepen our values; we only have to put the indigenous principles into practice, which is the more challenging part, and over time we will find that our values will change organically and we will feel compelled to shift our direction by enhancing meaning and purpose.

Chapter 21. Integrating Core Values

Life is like a path … and we all have to walk the path. As we walk, we'll find experiences like little scraps of paper in front of us along the way. We must pick up those pieces of scrap paper and put them in our pocket … Then one day, we will have enough scraps of papers to put together and see what they say. Read the information and take it to heart.

—Uncle Frank Davis (quoting his mother), Pawnee

This chapter will not provide a ten-point system for integrating core values, as integrating core values cannot be done through an intellectual process, a checklist, or by a motivational speaker hyping up the team. It must become a daily practice. In a sense, inculcating core values into a business culture is akin to the process of brand development, as modern brand evangelists are beginning to espouse.

The values, as with the brand, must permeate every aspect of a company. They cannot just be a grandiose statement, and we cannot just hire a top branding firm and expect them to do it for us. We have to live and breathe our values each and every day. We have to walk the talk, and that takes time and effort.

Yes, we do need to carefully articulate and communicate those values widely, place them on our website, talk through them with our teams, invite feedback and criticism, discuss how they can be applied to real-life situations, explore how strengthening our resolve to our values may affect our decision making, and so on. And yet, the real process of implementing core values is our daily practice.

We have all heard it said that if you change a behavior for twenty-one consecutive days, you can change a habit, yet twenty-one days is not necessarily enough time to solidify the new behavior in such a way that it will stick. Twelve-step programs, on the other hand, offer many parallels to the process of implementing indigenous principles and values systems. For example, it is advised to newcomers in recovery to attend ninety meetings in ninety days to rapidly and aggressively build a solid enough foundation of recovery to truly stay away from destructive substances before one can back off the frequency of attendance. In this they are applying the principle of the warrior spirit and also vigilance, which is a topic we'll cover in chapter 23.

In addition to the twelve steps of recovery programs, they also have twelve traditions and twelve principles. In fact, many people credit the long-standing continued success of twelve-step programs to their adherence to the twelve traditions, which read much like a value system. And with regard to their principles, they have a most important slogan: "Practice these principles in all our affairs," with the emphasis on "all." This is a central theme of indigenous culture, as well, in that there is no separation between how we live and how we generate our livelihood; it is all interrelated.

The process of implementing core values is much the same as the ninety meetings in ninety days concept, that we have to work a program of introspection, spending time with nature, spending time with elders, for men to spend time appreciating the unique qualities and strengths of women and for women to spend time appreciating the unique qualities and strengths of men, considering the interconnected nature of things, practicing being patient, practicing intentionality, deeply considering our integrity in all things, practicing thinking very long-term, and always striving to be a warrior—in essence practicing each of the indigenous principles explored in this book.

To begin implementing core values, we will have already deeply explored and identified what our values are, then we will communicate them, and then we will practice them daily in our lives and work. Publicly proclaiming our core values, as in publishing them on our website and stating them to our teams, will catalyze our efforts forward, so long as we continue to follow through.

It's much the same as a traditional wedding ceremony in that weddings have historically been just as much about proclaiming to a community that two individuals are indeed married and therefore unavailable to others, as about a ceremonial connection between a man and a woman. In most indigenous cultures, wedding ceremonies are pretty simple, given the primary purpose of public proclamation. Once the proclamation has been made, any continued flirtations on the part of either the husband or wife will be frowned upon in the community, and the community therefore is in support of the continued sanctity of their union. The wedding ring is also a constant reminder to all that a person is taken and unavailable.

Much the same way with publicly proclaimed values, once we go public, we are committed. When we go public to our employees and invite their feedback and criticisms, we are committed to living up to our values, and when we live up to our values, we are also in a position to hold our teams to those values. This is not to say that we function from a place of identifying failures and punishing people for them; rather, we should identify where we fall short of our values as an organization and explore how we can learn from those failings. It is important to recognize that we as leaders will be learning right along with our teams and colleagues, and we need to be understanding of the challenges others face related to implementing values.

If we can have the courage to speak openly of our own shortfalls in holding to our value system, what we have learned from them, and how we are striving to do better, we will have created the space for our employees to do the same. Living and working by a value system is going to represent a very different way of being and doing for many people. For many of us, it is not something that we will just instinctively know how to do, which is why we must continually practice it.

Practice, fail, talk it through, learn, and try again.

As stated at the outset, integrating core values is not something we do through an intellectual process or a checklist; it is achieved through a migration from an intellectually based system of leadership to a heart-based process of leadership, a process of leadership in which we *feel* our way through situations. We ask ourselves if our decisions *feel* right according to our values. Does our brand stand for something that *feels* good to us? Do we *feel* like we are living and working by our values?

If we want to track things such as sales metrics, expense trending, or supply-chain dynamics, we use our intellect. The decisions we make based on our findings need to merge our analytical thinking with our heart-based feelings and values. People are not numbers on spreadsheets. Spreadsheets are powerful tools to assist us in making informed decisions, yet we must always employ our feeling heart-based side as the final measurement. As the indigenous elders would tell us, people are sacred, and so is all of nature. They tell us that women are sacred life-givers, that to put ourselves in peril for a greater good is a sacred thing. They tell us that humility is a great attribute. They tell us to take care of our families *and* our communities. They tell us that listening intently is showing respect. And above all, they tell us to respect nature and our place within it.

Implementing core values is a continual process of change and evolution, from mind to heart, from analysis to compassion, and from serving profit to serving holism. It is about digging deeply into our own psychology, the basis of our thinking and decision making, and being willing to challenge ourselves and each other.

On the surface, it seems simple. Aren't values such as integrity, respecting diversity, and sustainability self-evident? Don't we already know we have good intentions? Why do we need to question ourselves? Perhaps for some individuals, these things are self-evident, and all that is needed is to hone their values and communicate them outwardly. Perhaps for some, they are already living them fully. Amen to those individuals. Yet what I have found is that values and our core intentions that drive our values are not so cut-and-dried. I'm not necessarily a big fan of Freud, but he did codify the deeply complex nature of the subconscious mind and identified our abilities for self-deception.

I recently met with a friend over coffee who was expressing dismay at the present state of her career. She had made much more money in the past, and at the time was only just getting by. So I asked her if her bills were being paid, to which she replied yes, and she also expressed that she was really enjoying her job. I suggested that she see the gift in her present job and choose gratitude over disappointment, to which she responded, "At my age and being single, I should be doing a lot better than this." Then I asked her what it was about her age and the fact that she was single that told her how much money she should be making, to which she did not have much of a response. The answer, of course, was that was her mental tape, a deeply seated subconscious belief that drove her mental and emotional discomfort around the state of her career at that point in time.

So in relation to her values, given her deep-seated belief system around her age and marital status, her intention was clouded by something so deep inside that she was not fully aware of, and if her intention was clouded, then her values were also in question. Deep-seated belief systems will inevitably cloud our values, and therein lies the challenge of maintaining authenticity. Why? Because as she works to evolve and transform her career, instead of following her true passions, she has a constant dialog running in her mind that dictates what she should and should not be doing and how much money she should or should not be making. Her belief system is so strong that her internal dialog lacks clarity.

For myself, I often get asked to speak at events or in ceremonial environments, to share songs or prayers, and sometimes to conduct ceremonies. If my intention in doing so is truly to help people, then I need to go inward to make sure there is no inkling of self-motivation, that there is no part of myself that is enjoying being the center of attention, receiving accolades, or being someone whom others look to for knowledge and wisdom. Most importantly, in ceremonial environments, I know that if I bring any amount of my own ego into it, I will be lessening the power of the blessings that are being requested from the ceremony, I will be interfering with the flow of energy from the spirit world, and in essence, I will be watering down the ceremony. Therefore, in ceremony, it is highly important that I maintain a place of crystal clear intention so that I can be in a place of complete service to the people coming for healing and the help that has been requested, which requires a constant dialog with the spirit world to stay in check.

As stated in chapter 10, ceremony is the gateway to intentionality; it is the underlying lesson to be learned—not the only lesson, but certainly the most powerful. One elder I have sat with in ceremony is widely noted for saying, "However you see your life being, that's how it's going to be." He says this over and over again so people won't forget it, as it is a statement that is much too easily glossed over as sounding like a mere platitude. This elder truly gets how powerful ceremony can be when practiced from a place of pure intention, and does his best to convey this teaching any chance he gets. And yet ceremonies are also a way of practicing for daily living, which is a major point of indigenous wisdom that is most often overlooked and relates very directly to the process of implementing core values; we practice in ceremony to implement in our daily lives.

The true medicine people are the ones who are in constant dialog with the spirit world and have achieved the state of walking in beauty. They are seen as walking in beauty because they are continuously in a place of pure intention, continuously exuding values of love, compassion, integrity, and connection with every word they speak and every gesture they make. These medicine people are magical to be in the presence of, and in a similar measure, as we increase the clarity of our intention, we too can achieve a magical state of existence.

Through clarity of intention, our sense of personal connection to our stated value system strengthens, as well as our clarity for daily implementation of those values, and the values become a part of the fiber of our being. In this place we do not need much analysis to arrive at decisions that are the right thing to do. We will instinctively know what to do and how to respond in every difficult situation we face.

At the outset of this chapter, I said there is no checklist for implementing core values, yet there is a process. The difference is that the process needs to be worked like a program, continuously, vigilantly, and with clarity of intention. The process is also circular, that is to say, without beginning or ending; it is continuous. If we practice it earnestly and consistently, it *will* work, and we *will* evolve our values, and from that evolution our culture *will* shift.

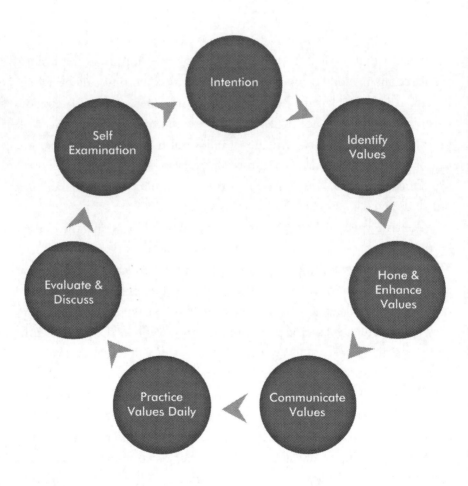

Chapter 22. The Lesson from Tobacco

Whenever you take anything from the Earth, remember to leave an offering.

—Joe Coyhis, Stockbridge-Munsee

When we want to talk to Him we burn tobacco and it takes our prayers all the way up to the Sky World.

—Louis Farmer, Onondaga

Tobacco in our modern culture is one of the most misunderstood of natural elements and also one of the most abused. Beginning with the peace pipe, as it is widely referred to in North America, is a misnomer in that North American indigenous people do not refer to their pipes in this way. While I debated the inclusion of this chapter, as it may seem somewhat redundant to earlier chapters on communication and integrity, the lesson from tobacco is important for the sake of coming to a deeper understanding of indigenous culture.

The use of sacred substances such as tobacco, sage, cedar, sweet grass, and so many other plant medicines is integral to their value system in that their use brings about a very tangible and physical connection to the plant world. In the burning of these medicines, one seeks purification, healing, and blessings from the smoke, and in so doing enters into a relationship with the plant world. To the indigenous, these relationships are very real and are to be respected and revered. Tobacco, as this chapter will illustrate, is the most powerful of these medicines according to the majority of North American indigenous people, and in light of such an understanding, it can be understood that tobacco is also sacred.

In the days of the Indian wars, the US government would send emissaries and military leaders to negotiate treaties with the Natives for the purpose of obtaining land and controlling Indian movements. As the emissaries sat with representatives from the Indian nations, the indigenous ones would begin by bringing out a pipe to smoke with the emissaries. Since the emissaries noticed that this practice always occurred when they sat to discuss peace with the Indians, they began referring to the pipe as the peace pipe.

The more interesting part of this story is that the reason the Natives brought out their pipes to smoke with the government officials is because their understanding of the purpose of tobacco is that when you use it intentionally, anything that you speak out loud will be heard by the Great Spirit. Whenever North American indigenous people want to speak words in such a way that people will hear not just their words, but also the intent of their heart, they will use tobacco to seal their words and make their intentions known. It is understood that lying while using tobacco in this way is something that is so dangerous that no one would be foolish enough to do so, as it is as if a person would be lying to the Creator.

To a non-Indian or those with little exposure to indigenous culture, this might seem like a nice custom; they might view it as something that came about over time to ensure honest communication. We might even say it's a beautiful ritual or see it as a trait of nobility.

To indigenous people, this is not merely a custom or ritual; rather, it is a knowing that they have of one of the most sacred of plant medicines. Natives know that if they use tobacco intentionally and lie or cheat a person, harm, possibly even great harm, will come to them, because they have disrespected the Holy Ones.

It was a brilliant thing for those chiefs and community leaders to invite the US government officials to smoke the pipe with them, as while those emissaries were unaware of what they were getting themselves into, the Indians would be able to observe the results in the lives of those who touched the pipe to their lips and took the tobacco into their lungs. If they lied, if they cheated, the Indians would see it in the outcome, which is not to say that the Indians would prevail politically and retain their lands and culture, but that bad things would come to those who misused the sacred tobacco.

In my life whenever there are really important words to be shared with people in our spiritual community, we say it with tobacco. When my wife and I got married, we spoke our vows with tobacco. When we are troubled about things, we roll a smoke and pray and talk with it, and it helps us find clarity.

However, I am not advocating that everyone take up smoking, as habitual use of store-bought tobacco is very harmful to your health. In our case, we are very careful not to purchase store-bought cigarettes, given the chemical additives they contain. We do not smoke tobacco with filters made of fiberglass. We purchase or are gifted organic tobacco, sometimes homegrown, and roll it ourselves, and most importantly we do not utilize it habitually.

The lesson we can take from this is not related to the use of tobacco necessarily, because one does not need to smoke tobacco to have honest intentional communication; one only needs to intend to speak with honesty and clarity. The lesson is that North American indigenous people have a specific formality that involves tobacco, which is for the purpose of entering into completely honest intentional communication.

When there are grievances, disagreement, or impasse, traditional indigenous people do not attempt to avoid, manipulate, or overpower; rather, they sit in calmness together. They listen carefully without interruption; they speak respectfully and from the heart with the intent of finding truth and making the truth known. Truth and harmony among the people is so important to their culture that they have evolved this method of communicating, together with the formality of tobacco, to ensure that it is completely honest and true.

Many Native people consider tobacco to be the strongest of plant medicines in terms of its ability to connect a person with Spirit. They don't use sassafras or licorice root to communicate, and yet they are both considered to have medicinal properties; rather, they use the strongest of medicine when it comes to communication because they value honest communication to be of the highest importance.

As most of what we do in business is communication of one form or another, how would we do things differently if we valued honesty above all else? If instead of maneuvering through interpersonal problems with the people we work with, what if we intended to speak with them with clarity and honesty, and to listen to them wholeheartedly?

This is an important lesson related to the integration of indigenous principles, as when we begin to shift corporate culture in a direction that incorporates these principles, or for that matter, when we begin to shift culture in any direction, there are going to be those who will resist and fight the changes, as many of us are creatures of habit and resist change of any kind.

Change can be painful, yet as nearly all the thought leaders who speak on innovation will say, it is necessary to keep an organization fresh, relevant, and healthy. So as we work to integrate our core values, even as we keep the focus on our own need to change, our changing will effect organizational change, and organizational change will bring about conflict and resistance. The best way I know to deal with this kind of conflict and resistance is with honest intentional communication.

One other piece of this lesson is also to communicate with gentleness and listen with an open mind and heart. When we speak intentionally and are clear within ourselves of what our intention is, we do not need to raise our voices or overpower. We can listen to people with views that are 180 degrees opposed to our own and not feel threatened. We can just listen and perceive their perspective, and as we perceive their perspective, we will discover how best to communicate with them.

You can envision you are smoking a sacred pipe or a rolled smoke with corn husk while you communicate, and together with your intention, it will have the same effect as if you were actually using tobacco. Or you can just gather your intention, state your purpose at the outset of the conversation, and ask permission to communicate in an honest way. Either the conflict will subside, or you will see the true intentions of others that are in conflict with your organization's core values, and you will know what to do.

Honesty, clarity, intentionality, and active listening, together with compassion and gentleness, comprise the lesson from tobacco.

Chapter 23. Vigilance

When you begin a great work you can't expect to finish it all at once; therefore, you and your brothers press on and let nothing discourage you until you have entirely finished what you have begun.

—Teedyuschung, Delaware

It is an obvious truth that if you want to get into top physical condition, you have to be willing to do the work, to exercise regularly and consistently, to eat wholesome foods, to seek expert advice, to learn to listen to the nuanced messages your body is telling you—when to step up your routine, when to back off, when to keep going. In short, you have to work at it and be willing to sacrifice for the benefit of the goal. The same obvious truth can be said for being an effective leader, which is that to be innovative, to work vigorously with creativity, passion, and integrity, takes constant effort.

What is the nature of this effort? Does that mean we work vigorously to control the behaviors of others, to look at reorganizations, hiring and firing, improvements in strategy, focusing on our brand, production, and distribution? Yes, we do all of these things, and yet the essence of what indigenous principles have to offer us is that the real work is internal.

It has been said, and I have absolutely found this to be true, that if we keep the focus on ourselves, meaning to constantly look at our behaviors, attitudes, belief systems, ways of communicating, and trigger points, for example, all the external conditions in our lives will fall beautifully into place. It has also been said that we move toward that which we think. So if we are constantly in a place of distrust or resentment, then we will draw distrust and resentment to us; we will manifest the conditions that give us justification for our distrust and resentment. The same is also true for constantly being in a place of trust, visioning, and passion; we will draw those fruits to ourselves as well.

Let us take a simple example. We have a sales organization that is faltering. We regularly call in our sales director and ask for the justifications for the revenue decline and ask him or her what the plan is for turning it around. Each time the sales director provides elaborate reasons for the decline that make perfect sense, that sound reasonable, as well as their strategies for improvement. So we send him or her away, thinking that he or she will turn it around, yet each time the numbers continue to decline and our frustration builds.

Is the problem that we need a new sales director? Maybe. Maybe the sales director is in over his or her head and doesn't really know what to do to turn it around, yet feels the need to come up with a story of how he or she will do it.

Or perhaps the problem is that the sales director does not fully understand or appreciate the real vision for the company. Perhaps he or she doesn't fully believe in our vision. Or perhaps he or she doesn't respect us or believe in us as a leader he or she can stand behind. Perhaps he or she is resentful about the compensation package, or really knows that our industry is in for big changes, but doesn't care to tell us. Or perhaps his or her people management skills are really bad, and the sales organization is in open revolt.

The problem and the solution could be anything, yet what is the first tendency we lean toward as leaders? Do we react by beating down on the sales director, telling him or her he or she needs to sell more? Do we naively accept his or her story and work in the blind, constantly worrying about the numbers? Do we begin to distrust the sales director and look for examples that justify our distrust? Do we start thinking that we need to reorganize the sales group? Do we look for his or her replacement and think that that will solve the problem?

Or do we listen carefully and thoughtfully to the sales director, asking questions for clarity, putting ourselves in the sales director's shoes when listening, and looking for signs of sincerity? Are we then willing to both consider the validity of the sales director's story and also look beyond his or her story to incorporate all levels of things that affect our sales organization? Most importantly, are we willing to look at our own part in the problem? Have we not been spending enough time with the sales director, speaking with him or her more about the long-term vision for the company and where the product is going, the values and ethics of the organization, or perhaps taking to heart his or her concerns about distribution, customer service, or internal resources?

In short, do we apply a nuanced approach to the problem that includes a willingness to consider our own part?

The first set of examples represent an external approach; the second set implies an internal process of self-checking and personal responsibility. To take an example from the world of recovery, it is a well-known behavior pattern for some in recovery to think that if they move, change jobs, change friends and relationships, they will get clean and sober and their life will improve. There are many people with a history of moving around the country thinking things will get better, and things *will* improve a little at first, thus providing continued justification for the constant upheaval. Yet the laws of physics, if you will, are such that if you do not change the conditions that created the problem in the first place, the problem will eventually recur. Or as Buckaroo Banzai once said, "No matter where you go, there you are."

There is a great tendency among leaders to look at the external factors in their organizations and point to the deficiencies in those factors as being the primary impetus for lackluster performance. I have seen large organizations go through round after round of layoffs and reorganizations thinking that things will improve. Each reorg the e-mail goes out something to the effect of "So and so is being promoted to such and such position and will be responsible for such and such, and so and so is transferring to such and such …" And all of these changes are characterized as "better enabling us to leverage strategic advantages, improve production, reduce costs," and so on. They might as well be saying that by shuffling the deck, we will end poverty, heal the sick, save the environment, and have peace on Earth.

It won't work, unless and until the physical changes are a reflection and an extension of the internal work that has been done on the part of the highest levels of executives in the organization—genuine, thoughtful, and heartfelt internal work that results in what quantum physics refers to as quantum nonlocality, or a quantum leap in understanding that brings about an almost immediate awareness of how an organization needs to change in order to realize its potential in the world.

So here is where vigilance comes in.

These internal changes do not come easy. Nor do they come all at once. They come from a continuous process of introspection, self-examination, and a willingness to consider one's own shortcomings. Not only will our own changes result in better performance on our own part, but they will also engender a willingness within our organizations to accept personal responsibility. Our people will be more willing to take calculated risks and own their failures. They will be more willing to work in collaboration. They will be more willing to consider the perspectives of others. They will work as a true team and also become autonomous. They will respect us like we have never known respect, and they will want with every fiber of their being to make *their* company successful. In essence, their behavior will reflect our own.

There is a reason that all great things require continuous consistent effort, why getting into shape means regular exercise and eating better, being a PhD requires years of schooling, being a CEO requires years of experience, and so on. The continuous constant effort and years of labor also result in the attainment of the wisdom required to responsibly wield our newfound abilities. Except in rare cases of extreme genius, I have never found shortcuts to truly work in the long run. One great slogan I have heard is "Half measures avail us nothing."

One could take steroids and hire a personal trainer and get ripped quickly, but then there are serious physical side effects from taking steroids. So would such a person really be in top physical condition, or would he or she have just created a new problem to solve another? One could trump up a PhD, hire an amazing ghostwriter, and bill himself or herself out as an effective strategist, but how far would that really take a person? You get the idea.

As for being an effective visionary leader, there are many examples of individuals who have relied on a family name, an Ivy League education, personal connections, and alliances formed with key people, and now find themselves running large organizations. Perhaps some of these individuals are actually good at it or became good at it over time—more power to them if so.

The point is, to truly be good at it, one needs to become a long-term student of leadership, not just thoroughly learning the external factors of running a company, but also the internal dimensions of one's own motivations, fears, and shortcomings, as well as one's unique qualities, talents, and passions—what a person uniquely brings to the table that gives fire to an organization.

The example that we draw from indigenous culture related to vigilance is first and foremost their ceremonies. In every example I have seen of indigenous ceremonies, they are all physically demanding. They require fasting, sleep deprivation, exposure to extremes of temperature as in sitting in extremely hot sweat lodges feeling like you're being parboiled. There are even ceremonies such as the Sun Dance that require the piercing of flesh and carving flesh offerings from one's arms to offer as a demonstration of the seriousness of the practitioner's prayers.

Don't worry. I'm not suggesting to the reader to start carving flesh or taking brutally hot showers, but as I have learned over many years of participating in these ceremonies, everything, absolutely everything in these ceremonies is intentional. There are important reasons for everything that takes place within the ceremonies, principal among them that the willingness of the practitioners is a constant, steady, determined demonstration of their commitment to connect themselves with the spirit world for the sake of humbly asking for blessings for the benefit of their families, their communities, and their lives.

Over years of participating in these ceremonies with earnestness, fortitude, and sincerity, one becomes very strong, strong enough to face any of life's challenges with equanimity. One also becomes wise, wise enough to know when and how to use the power of one's mental and emotional strength for the greater good. With wisdom also comes the ability to mentor and guide others in their dedication to spiritual exploration and personal transformation.

It always comes down to the individual, how far the individual takes it, how much wisdom he or she will derive from the practice, what his or her intentions are, and how his or her prayers are directed. Not all who dedicate themselves to a lifelong practice of indigenous ceremonies attain the same level of wisdom. The difference comes from the intention of each individual.

However, if a person's intention is to become truly wise for the benefit of his or her family, community, and humanity, to become in service to humanity, and to maintain a strong vigilance to not let his or her ego get in the way, it is highly likely that he or she will one day become a true elder, to reach the point we explored in chapter 7 in which a person walks in beauty, that every word, gesture, and action is in beauty, and as one elder expressed, will achieve unspeakable joy.

To apply this to our goal of becoming inspirational, innovative, effective leaders, it starts with a clear intention, followed by a continuous practice of self-examination and introspection, a ceremony if you will, the act of honoring ourselves for all that is both admirable and without merit, being willing to change our belief systems and attitudes, letting go of resentments and fears. As Gandhi famously said, "You must be the change you wish to see in the world."

In my own process, what I have discovered is not just all the areas I need to change and things I need to let go of, but I have also come into a more full sense of the gifts that I have to offer the world, my true talents, the contents of my heart, and a clear feeling of where my true motivations lie. The result has been a deeper understanding and relationship with myself and a deeper self-love and self-respect.

Yet the process never stops. I don't reach a point where I can say, "I got this," and then coast. We sometimes might feel the need or desire to plateau for a spell, to coast on the work we've done, but the shorter we stay on the plateau the better, lest we become too comfortable with our present state of being and become prone again to seeing the challenges around us as having to do with others.

This work is not easy, but the results are immeasurably gratifying and fulfilling and bring about far more than we could have otherwise imagined possible. It is the same as with indigenous ceremonies, in that being so physically challenging, they are simple but not easy, and so they tend to draw the serious ones, those who are truly committed to growth, for those are the ones who are worthy of the gifts that come from such a life's path.

As I see it, I believe that both heaven and hell exist right here on Earth, in the constructs of our own minds; we can make our lives miserable or beautiful based on how we think and feel. I also believe that we are presently on a precipice of change, an opportunity to reshape the world in which we exist. Through the immediacy of the Internet and the speed with which information flows in our present day, we can share insights, know-how, and wisdoms in an experiential format and instantly reach the four corners of the globe.

We also have the ability to reshape the working world one company at a time, one leader at a time, and each company has the ability to light the way for countless others to follow. We have the ability to create a paradise on Earth, to transform our addiction to fear and ego into a beingness of gratitude, acceptance, and trust. It starts with us, and it grows relative to our vigilance to constantly look at ourselves, our part to play, our role as a change agent, an agent of goodness, a mentor, and a beacon of vision for others to follow.

Beginning with ourselves, continuing with our vigilance, assisted and supported with trust, as we shall explore in the next chapter, I will leave you with one final thought on the topic of vigilance, a quote from Helen Keller.

> Character cannot be developed in ease and quiet. Only through experience of trial and suffering can the soul be strengthened, ambition inspired, and success achieved.

Chapter 24. Trust

The greater the faith, the greater the result.
—Fools Crow, Lakota

Learning to trust completely is where the exploration of indigenous principles moves into a mystical dimension. This is not an intellectual principle, and yet it can bring about great powers of the mind. It is not so much about trusting in a higher power as it is about trusting in a process.

One thing many of us tend to be very good at, myself included up until this current phase in my life, is doubting ourselves. We can have great moments of clarity, feel resonance with a current path, even see some positive results from our efforts, but as soon as the going gets tough or we run into conflict or someone comes into our office telling us we have it all wrong, we start to question ourselves and our process.

It is an absolute truth that we are far better off always being willing to look at ourselves, our shortcomings, our weaknesses, and vigilantly look for flaws in our strategies and plans, which also means being open to criticism. Yet at the same time and on a different level, we must also hold true to ourselves, never forgetting who we are and what our strengths and talents are.

Since change is an uncomfortable process for nearly everyone, anytime we bring about change, there will be those who will resist and criticize. One excellent example is how Thomas Edison famously and publicly ridiculed Nicola Tesla, the inventor of alternating current. Edison developed the less efficient and clunky direct current electric engine, which at the time was powering the entire world. So rather than succumbing to the fact that Tesla had invented a superior technology and accepting that its use would be a better course for humanity, he publicly electrocuted animals in town squares using Tesla's alternating current engine as a demonstration of the dangers of the technology.[1] People fell for this gimmickry for some time; however, fortunately for us, today we can power our world with the more efficient alternating current. Yet Tesla was a casualty of resistance to change as his career was continually plagued by skepticism and doubt.

Great leaders are known for stubbornly adhering to a particular strategy and vision, seemingly at all costs and in the face of great opposition. They hold a vision in their mind, they can see it taking form, and they work tirelessly to remove all obstacles to making their vision a reality. Trust is a big part of what drives them—trust in themselves and trust in their vision. Perhaps their methods may at times be messy, yet they can see the future and work toward that end without a doubt in their minds as to the efficacy of their vision. History has given us many examples of great things created by visionary leaders who knew the importance of trust.

Many of us, myself included up until a previous phase in my life, are also good at self-deception. This is the other side of trust. If we stubbornly adhere to our ideas, strategies, and plans and think that all those who criticize them are the ones with the problem, then we are on a crash course for disaster. We can hold the notion that we are good communicators, that we treat people equally with respect, that we are balanced, that we do not lean toward manipulation, and so on, which is a mind-set that can enable us to deceive ourselves into thinking that all the problems stem from other people. As we have already thoroughly covered this concept previously, I won't belabor the point, except to say that there is a fine line between conviction in one's vision and confidence in one's strengths and abilities, and an unwillingness to face one's shortcomings.

Therefore, vigilance and trust are close partners in the process of integrating paradigm shift: vigilance, to constantly be questioning our motives, our tactics, our ethics, our vision, our strategy, and all—and trust, to constantly be reminding ourselves who we are and what we are about.

This is an important distinction to master. We can practice our process of self-questioning, and then as we do so, ask ourselves how the questioning feels. Does it feel like we are beating ourselves up? Does it feel like we are thinking critically? Does it feel like we are defending ourselves from our detractors, being in defensive mode? Does it feel oddly uncomfortable, yet truthful? Do we feel anger? Do we feel confidence? Do we feel confirmed, validated, or justified?

We need both vigilance to keep self-checking, and trust to continue the process.

This is a subtle process and can take years to master, and yet these two concepts are critically important to the continual evolution of our mastery of leadership.

To take this topic to a deeper level, let me illustrate with a description of the Sun Dance ceremony. Sun Dance is generally understood to be a Lakota ceremony, yet there are many other tribes that practice this ceremony as well. There are also similar ceremonies that other tribes hold within their own traditions, such as the enemy way ceremony of the Navajo, the stomp dance conducted by the Cherokee, or the smoke dance of the Iroquois.

As described in chapter 6, the Sun Dance ceremony takes place in a large arbor, open to the sun in the middle, ringed with a covered area. In the center is what is referred to as the tree of life, a cottonwood tree with two main branches forming a fork from the trunk. The tree is carefully selected, prayed over, offerings given, cut down by hand tool, taken into the arbor, and erected on what is referred to as tree day, the day before the dance begins.

Sun Dancers commit themselves typically to a minimum of four years of participation in the ceremony, and the ceremony lasts for eight days, four days of purification followed by four days of the dance itself. In some traditions, the dance is also followed by another four days of reverence, in which aspects of the ceremony continue on.

There is a huge amount of preparation that goes into a Sun Dance ceremony. Sun Dancers not only commit themselves to participating in a ceremony, but to a way of life. They undergo huge personal sacrifices to participate, many times quitting jobs so they can make it to ceremony, sometimes getting there on a whim and a prayer. The preparations go on throughout the year and build to this one time of year in which the ceremony takes over their lives.

On a physical level, the Sun Dance requires a huge personal sacrifice. Beginning when the tree of life is erected in the arbor, dancers do not take food or water until the four days of the dance have completed. They rise before dawn and enter into a sweat-lodge ceremony, in which hot rocks are brought in, water is poured on them which produces steam, songs are sung and prayers are spoken. Right at dawn they dance into the arbor and begin round after round of dancing throughout the hot summer days, many times in the range of ninety degrees and above, facing the sun, dancing barefoot on the ground. Then a little before sundown, they dance out of the arbor and go back into the sweat lodge for another two rounds of singing, praying, and sweating, and repeat the process for four days.

Most people of reasonable to good physical conditioning who dance in the sun in ninety-plus-degree weather for four days without food or water, participate in a sweat ceremony at dawn and dusk losing more hydration, and do so out of the context of a ceremony that stretches back for a thousand years or more would likely die of exposure before the four days were up. And did I mention the piercing of flesh and the giving of flesh offerings?

Yet Sun Dancers do not perish during these ceremonies. They are a little weary afterward, yet typically get back in their cars, drive hundreds of miles home, take a good long shower, go to bed, and get up and go to work the next day. Their survival comes from the giving over of their lives fully to the ceremony, and a complete and absolute trust in the construct of the ceremony, which includes the presence and help of the spirit world to carry them through safely.

To draw another analogy from recovery, as I see many similarities between twelve-step and indigenous ceremonies, there are a couple of slogans that you will hear around twelve-step people, namely, "We don't know how it works; we just know that it works" and "It works if you work it." Herein lies the mystery. We can't say exactly why Sun Dancers don't perish during the course of their ordeal, yet it sure seems powerfully evident to me that having complete trust and a complete willingness to turn one's life over to a higher power results in something mystical. I have seen it in all the ceremonies I have participated in.

Therefore, the lesson from the indigenous is that placing our trust, not blind trust, but knowing, intentional trust, in something greater than ourselves, with a noble set of values, with a vision that brings about energy, passion, and excitement, will, by the nature of the construct, bring about a magical, mystical evolution in our adventure called running a business.

As leaders, we are tasked with the formation and refinement of the construct; the construct is the industry, the product or service, followed by the value system, communicated as a vision, consisting of unique individuals—all of which embodied together becomes a business. As we shape and refine the construct and then trust completely in the process, which includes the values and the people, and if we follow the lessons from the ancient teachings—we respect Earth, we honor the aliveness of all things, we respect the wisdom of those who have come before us, we see that we are all connected, we exercise great patience, we have clear intention, we respect all people, we think in terms of the impact of our efforts on the seventh generation unborn, we speak and listen carefully, we employ the highest of ethics, and we come from the heart—together with the warrior spirit, values, purpose, vigilance, trust, and humility, we will achieve great things.

Chapter 25. Humility

For me, the essence of a medicine man's life is to be humble, to have great patience, to be close to the Earth, to live as simply as possible, and to never stop learning.

—Archie Fir Lame Deer, Lakota

Humility, as is the way of love, the principle explored in chapter 14, is another byproduct of the employment of indigenous principles. It is not so much a principle, but rather a measure of one's success in the attainment of understanding and mastery of the traditions. When we see an elder of true humility, we know that this is an elder who has walked the talk for a very long time.

At the halfway point in a ceremony I sponsored in August 2007, the ceremony described in chapters 8 and 10, there was a defining moment. It was at the point that we call for midnight water, in which the singing and drumming pauses, the fireman brings in a bucket of water, places it before the fire, rolls a smoke of corn husk and tobacco, and begins to speak and then pray with the smoke. When the fireman is done with his prayer, the water bucket is passed around the tepee clockwise so that each person can take a drink of water, and as the bucket is being passed, it is common that the roadman, the person running the ceremony, will open up the ceremony for those who wish to speak to do so at that time.

It was at this time that I asked to speak and began addressing people around the tepee and expressing my gratitude for their contributions and presence in the ceremony. I had many nice things to say about these people, many of whom I had known for a number of years and had grown close with. After I had addressed about half the people in the tepee, I came to an individual, a close brother of mine in the community, who was sitting directly across from me, and began thanking him for some really amazing things he had done for me.

As I was thanking my brother, he cut me off and essentially told me to stop talking. He was indicating that at this time in the ceremony, I was not to take a lot of time talking and was instead to just quickly and simply say thank you. I responded to him that I was attempting to do just that, and he cut me off again, reiterating that this was not the time for me to speak so much.

As I looked quickly around the tepee, I noticed expressions of shock on the faces of some of the others, as they couldn't believe the scope of the breach of protocol my brother had just committed. One never interrupts a person when he or she has the floor in a tepee ceremony, especially not the sponsor, and most especially not when the sponsor is saying such nice things about people.

Yet what came over me in that moment, as I lost my train of thought and stopped talking, was a feeling that can only be described as the single greatest moment of humility of my life, a complete and full recognition that he was right. I was talking way too much and taking advantage of my status as the sponsor to dominate the attention of the tepee. I was also distracting attention from the original purpose of the ceremony, which was in fact my own purpose of emotional healing and massive life change.

It was at this moment that I felt a sensation almost as if water were trickling down my body, beginning from the top of my head all the way to my toes. I slumped into the blankets I was sitting on, and I went to a deeply internal place of self-examination.

It is said that in ceremony, in particular a ceremony in which a person is the sponsor, everything that takes place is a reflection of your life, and all we have to do is pay careful attention to all the signs, indications, and goings-on to be intimately informed about how our lives are, what we need to let go of, and what we need to be in peace about. What this interruption brought about was a deep realization of the times in my life when dominating discussion was more important to me than real progress.

How many times do we do this as leaders? How many times do we assume that we know something merely because of our position and experience or dominate meetings and discussions because we feel we must, as leaders, be the center of everything?

Even though my brother was spot-on right and his interruption was exactly what I needed at the time, he felt terrible about his breach of protocol and left the ceremony. Upon noticing this, the roadman sent the cedarman to go bring him back. When he came back, he was given a short minute to apologize to me and throw some cedar on the coals, and then the roadman instructed the next singer to begin the next set of songs. I was not given an opportunity to respond, and again I was shown the great wisdom of this on the part of the roadman in that at that point in the ceremony, it was more important to get back to a complete focus on the purpose of the ceremony. We could deal with words in the morning near the conclusion of the ceremony, but not then.

This feeling that had come over me put me into exactly the space I needed to be in to receive the healing, teachings, and blessing the ceremony had to offer, a space of complete, unadulterated humility. I did not need to express anything in that moment, just to be in that place and hold it throughout the ceremony.

Up until his interruption, we were all having a great ceremony, and many nice things had been said about me, to me, and by me to others. Everyone was feeling good. But that wasn't why we were there, and my brother's interruption enabled me to step back from the direction I was going in, sit for several hours in a place of profound humility, and then when I was ready, proceed forward again, in a new direction with a different way of being. I stepped into this ceremony as one man and came out in the morning another.

Many hours later as morning light approached, I had the opportunity to express to my brother that no apology was necessary, that he had given me a great healing with his words and his courage to use them at just the right moment. Although I think my brother would say that courage had nothing to do with it; I think he would say that he just opened his mouth and the words came out. Complete unadulterated humility was the defining moment of the ceremony and the new energy space that redirected my life in a new direction, a direction of healing and change.

It is a popular misconception of many that humility equates with weakness. This, I have found, could not be further from the truth. In a society that celebrates bravado, toughness, power, and aggression, these character traits, if looked at from a different perspective, can actually reflect weakness in a person.

What we can learn from the example of indigenous warriors is that they have consistently defined themselves in extraordinary ways in battle. Native American soldiers in the United States are among the most decorated of all. Geronimo was famously known for drawing the fire of the US Army and leading them into ambushes or away from his people, and yet Geronimo was also known among Indian people for practicing the same religion as the ceremony I've just described, a ceremony in which humility is the place we aspire to go in order to receive the blessings, guidance, and knowledge that flows from these ceremonies.

The now well-known battle cry of "It's a good day to die" came from the Indians and reflects the calm with which they would enter battle—quite different from proclamations used by our modern-day warriors of how they will "kick some ass," followed by the popular hooahs.

I am referencing the arena of war, as the act of entering battle knowing that you will be facing hundreds or perhaps thousands of people intent on killing you—and it is either you or them—is about the most frightening thing a person can do. How we tend to deal with it today in the United States is to pump up the soldiers and make them think they are the most-well-trained, best-equipped, and best soldiers in the world. We also heavily demonize their opponents so that they will feel morally justified.

The concept of the physical warrior, the one who fights a physical battle for the protection of people, land, or a way of life, is one that is also deeply engrained in indigenous culture. In all aspects of indigenous culture, the veteran is highly regarded and respected. There are special songs to honor them, special ceremonies to welcome them back into the community, special healing ceremonies to help them recover from the emotional wounds of battle, and they all hold a special status among the people.

Yet the nature of the respect in which they are held has nothing to do with how tough or fearless they are; rather, it honors the fact that they demonstrated a complete willingness to sacrifice themselves, their very lives if necessary, for the good of the people. Our US military does at times convey this same meaning to its soldiers, reflected in the use of the colloquialism of being in the service, indicating that being in the military is a form of being in service to society.

This concept of putting one's self in harm's way for the good of others is not exclusive to the image of a strong physical man; it is also what mothers do every day of their lives to protect and rear their children. In fact, this concept of being a warrior, as defined as *demonstrating a willingness to put one's self in harm's way for the good of others*, is a distinctly female character trait, as the feminine orientation is almost always directed toward the common good in the long term. This level of self-sacrifice is also about the most humble thing a person can do and yet demonstrates immeasurable strength and courage.

Therefore the learning we can take from indigenous culture is that the humble way is the strong way, and the way of overt displays of toughness shows weakness in that outward displays demonstrate a self-centered motivation for being tough.

Jean-François Zobrist, CEO of FAVI, a fifty-year-old French company that manufactures copper alloy automotive components, replied when asked what kind of a CEO he is, "I am a stupid and lazy manager." When Zobrist took over as CEO in 1983, he recognized that the current management of the company was top-down and that those doing the physical manufacturing work frequently commented that they didn't know anything and that decisions were consistently pushed to the highest levels. Zobrist immediately turned the management paradigm upside down by proclaiming the rank-and-file workers to be the experts and then gave them the autonomy needed to guide their own operations.[1]

Zobrist took a humble approach to management. He did not proclaim that because he is the CEO that he knows best; rather, he established himself as the headlights and the windshield of the organization, guiding its vision, being in support of the team, and ultimately leaving people alone to do what they know how to do best. As a result, FAVI has remained consistently successful, with a perfect service record, and Zobrist has remained at the helm for thirty years.

From the perspective of my indigenous training, I think Zobrist is far from stupid or lazy; rather, he is a true warrior, with humility, and a servant to his people. This, in essence, is an important message of this book in a nutshell: to endeavor to step away from the paradigm of self-serving status and recognition, to a paradigm of warrior leaders working as humble servants.

There is also a huge fringe benefit that comes with the cultivation of humility, and that is that incredible beauty can be found in the most unexpected of places. I cannot speak too much of specific things I have witnessed in ceremonies related to acts of humility, as they tend to be very personal. There are also specifics related to the ceremonial traditions that are better not written about, as they can only be experienced firsthand; otherwise they will be misunderstood. Suffice it to say, I have experienced profound moments of beauty and meaning through the witnessing of incredible acts of humility in others, and the greatest moments of joy I have experienced in my life have also been moments in which I have been able to reach a place of profound humility.

As a fringe benefit of practicing indigenous principles in all our affairs, the rewards are immeasurable and truly attainable for all.

Conclusion

Behold, my bothers, the spring has come; the earth has received the embraces of the sun and we shall soon see the results of that love!

—Sitting Bull, Sioux

The Medicine people focus on their Being, not their doing. After all, we are human beings not human doings. The Medicine people are very patient and consciously trying to live a life of humility. Medicine people are servant leaders. Their main purpose is to serve the needs of others. By this service attitude, they become the leaders people listen to and the leaders the people want to follow. The Medicine people say everyone is their teacher. Maybe we should try to live this way ourselves; humble, patient, honoring the Earth and listening to our teachers.

—From Elder's Meditation, June 16, 2012[1]

If there has been a consistent thread throughout this book and the thirteen indigenous principles explored herein, it is that we exist for a purpose far more vast and expansive than merely delivering profits. The principles, individually and collectively, show us a different way of being and doing in the world that brings us to a place of deeper meaning, and in that new or perhaps different way of being in the world with deeper meaning, abundance, prosperity, and fulfillment will naturally follow.

We know that if we jump off the roof of a building, we will fall and most likely perish. We know that if we place our hands in a fire, we will get burned. We do not argue with the laws of gravity or thermodynamics, and yet we have a continuous battle in our modern culture with the fundamental laws of existence. The indigenous elders speak of spiritual laws and the laws of nature. They see themselves as a part of a greater whole, not with dominion over, but in balance with. This is a natural law. Yet we think that we can be wasteful of natural resources, that we can pollute the environment, and that technology and science will solve our environmental problems.

We behave as though we can consume natural resources at a rate far greater than Mother Earth can replenish and that our scientists will come up with a solution for us. This is arguing with natural law and disrespecting the balance of nature. This is tantamount to jumping off a building and expecting to float. Sure, we can get away with environmental exploitation for a while, but sooner or later, the great equalizer of all, Mother Earth, will have her word with modern society. Some would argue that her word is already taking place with the rapidly melting glaciers, rising sea levels, and super storms.

It is also as if we are putting our hands in the fire and expecting that we will not burn, when we think that hierarchy may make us immune to the laws of decency and respect. I have heard one CEO in particular tell me that she felt that because she is a CEO, she can conduct herself with arrogance and people will be okay with it. For myself, there have been times in the past in which I have been hard on the people who worked for me because I was treating my position as though I had carte blanche to do so in order to ensure the needed results from the team. It does not matter if conduct that diminishes people comes from the CEO or the janitor; it still diminishes people and is out of balance with natural law.

When we reduce our reason for being in business to the sole objective of delivering profits, we are in essence diminishing people. We are saying that profit is more important than people, more important than being good human beings, respecting nature, respecting each other, and truly caring about the people we work with. When we work for profit alone, we are giving into an emotional condition that clouds our perception of the world. It prevents us from seeing and feeling the deeper meaning that we all want and crave in our lives, and reduces us to a smaller existence.

Our indigenous brothers and sisters, those who have retained the traditional teachings and knowledge, have known these things for thousands of years. It is engrained in their culture and way of being. They take it slow and patient; they have respect for the genders, for the elders, and for nature. They act with clear, well-thought-out intention, they value love in all their affairs, they see themselves as part of a whole, they consider their actions in relation to their very long-term effects, they speak the truth all the time, they choose their words carefully, they acknowledge the life in all things both animate and inanimate, and they acknowledge and respect the spirit world. They also, universally, respect the way of the warrior, as defined as a willingness to do what is right even when it is difficult.

When we are willing to compromise our values and ethics for the purpose of generating profits, or even to substitute our deeper desires and passions for doing the work we authentically love to do for the sake of revenue, we diminish our existence. The hammer and saw were made to serve the carpenter, just as business and commerce developed over time to serve humanity in the process of generating livelihood. It takes a warrior's spirit to rise above the bottom-line mantra of corporate culture and work for something more meaningful.

To end our exploration as we began, with a quote by Thomas Yellowtail, "Today, what is important for us is to realize that the old sacred ways are correct, and that if we do not follow them we will be lost and without a guide."[2]

These are all simple teachings. Not necessarily easy, but simple. It is when we fight with the laws of nature and the laws of life that we employ our intellectual and analytical powers to rationalize and justify jumping off a ledge with the expectation that we will float. If we spend so much of our time analyzing, debating, and arguing over how things should be, we will argue and debate ourselves right out of existence. The message from the medicine people is clear; it is that now is the time for being, feeling, and living with meaning and purpose.

Nizhoni.

Notes

Introduction:

1. David M. Raup, *Extinction: Bad Genes or Bad Luck?* (New York: Norton, 1992).
2. "Modern Slavery Statistics," Abolition Media, accessed January 14, 2014, http://abolitionmedia.org/about-us/modern-slavery-statistics.
3. "About Slavery," Free the Slaves, accessed January 14, 2014, http://www.freetheslaves.net/page.aspx?pid=348.
4. "How to Tackle U.S. Employees' Stagnating Engagement," *Gallup Business Journal*, June 11, 2013, http://businessjournal.gallup.com/content/162953/tackle-employees-stagnating-engagement.aspx.
5. Paul Hawken, *The Ecology of Commerce* (New York: HarperCollins Publishers, 1993), xiv.
6. Raj Sisodia, David B. Wolfe, and Jag Sheth, *Firms of Endearment* (Upper Saddle River, NJ: Wharton School Publishing, 2007).
7. Gary Hamel, *The Future of Management* (Boston: Harvard Business Press, 2007), 8.
8. Ibid., 255.
9. Seth Godin, *Tribes: We Need You to Lead Us* (New York: Penguin Group, 2008).
10. "Our Mission Statement," Grandmothers Council, accessed January 14, 2014, http://www.grandmotherscouncil.org/.

Chapter 3: At Its Core

1. F. Scott Fitzgerald, BrainyQuote.com, Xplore, accessed October 26, 2013, http://www.brainyquote.com/quotes/quotes/f/fscottfit100572.html.

Chapter 4: Indigenous Principles

1. Quoted in Norbert S. Hill Jr., *Words of Power: Voices From Indian America* (Golden, CO: Fulcrum Publishing, 1994), 5.

Chapter 5: Connection to Earth

1. Kyle Stock, "Patagonia's Confusing and Effective Campaign to Grudgingly Sell Stuff," BloombergBusinessweek, November 25, 2013, http://www.businessweek.com/articles/2013-11-25/patagonias-confusing-and-effective-campaign-to-grudgingly-sell-stuff.
2. "Common Threads Initiative," Patagonia, accessed January 14, 2014, http://www.patagonia.com/email/11/112811.html.

Chapter 6: Everything Is Alive

1. John F. Kennedy, BrainyQuote.com, Xplore, accessed November 29, 2013, http://www.brainyquote.com/quotes/quotes/j/johnfkenn121367.html.
2. Mahatma Gandhi, Mahatma.com, accessed January 14, 2014, http://www.mahatma.com/php/showNews.php?newsid=65&linkid=11
3. Henry Ford, BrainyQuote.com, Xplore, accessed November 29, 2013, http://www.brainyquote.com/quotes/quotes/h/henryford163828.html.
4. David Sheff, "Playboy Interview: Steven Jobs," *Playboy Magazine*, February 1, 1985, http://stevejobs.miranj.in/.

Chapter 8: The Four Directions

1. "Elder's Meditation," newsletter, June 26, 2012, http://whitebison.org/meditation/.

Chapter 9: Patience

1. Sisodia, Wolfe, and Sheth, *Firms of Endearment*.
2. Slavin, Kevin, "How Algorithms Shape Our World," TED video, 15:23, filmed July 2011, posted July 2011, http://www.ted.com/talks/kevin_slavin_how_algorithms_shape_our_world.html.

Chapter 10: Intentionality

1. Tony Hsieh, *Delivering Happiness: A Path to Profits, Passion, and Purpose* (New York: Business Plus, Hachette Book Group, 2010).

Chapter 11: Roles of Men and Women

1. Catalyst, "The Bottom Line: Corporate Performance and Women's Representation on Boards (2004–2008)," 2011 study http://www.catalyst.org/knowledge/bottom-line-corporate-performance-and-womens-representation-boards-20042008.
2. "Does Gender Diversity Improve Performance?," Credit-Suisse, July 31, 2012, https://www.credit-suisse.com/ch/en/news-and-expertise/research/credit-suisse-research-institute/news-and-videos.article.html/article/pwp/news-and-expertise/2012/07/en/does-gender-diversity-improve-performance.html.
3. Catalyst, "Advancing Women Leaders: The Connection Between Women Board Directors and Women Corporate Officers," 2008 study, http://www.catalyst.org/knowledge/advancing-women-leaders-connection-between-women-board-directors-and-women-corporate
4. Hsieh, *Delivering Happiness: A Path to Profits, Passion, and Purpose*, 183.

Chapter 12: Seventh Generation Unborn

1. Raup, *Extinction: Bad Genes or Bad Luck?*.

Chapter 14: The Way of Love

1. Hsieh, *Delivering Happiness: A Path to Profits, Passion, and Purpose*.

Chapter 15: Integrity

1. Jack Welch, *Winning* (New York: HarperCollins, 2005).

Chapter 16: The Spirit World

1. Albert Einstein, BrainyQuote.com, Xplore, accessed November 30, 2013, http://www.brainyquote.com/quotes/quotes/a/alberteins165188.html.

2. Michele Toomey, "Liberated Theology: Building on Einstein's View of God," 2009, http://www.mtoomey.com/EinsteinViewOfGod.html.

Chapter 19: Creating Purpose

1. Sisodia, Wolfe, and Sheth, *Firms of Endearment*.
2. "About Us," Hot Dog on a Stick, accessed January 14, 2014, http://www.hotdogonastick.com/aboutUs.aspx.

Chapter 20: Creating Core Values

1. Wiki Answers, "What Was Enron's Mission Statement?," accessed January 14, 2014,http://wiki.answers.com/Q /What_was_Enron's_mission_statement.
2. Meridith Elliott Powell, *Winning in the Trust and Value Economy* (London: Global Professional Publishing, 2013), 5.

Chapter 24: Trust

1. "Edison Electrocutes Elephant," accessed January 14, http://www.lateralscience.co.uk/electrocution/.

Chapter 25: Humility

1. Matthew E. May, "Mastering the Art of Bosslessness," FastCompany.com, September 26, 2012, http://www.fastcompany .com/3001574/mastering-art-bosslessness?partner=newsletter.

Conclusion

1. "Elder's Meditation," newsletter, June 16, 2012, http://whitebison.org/meditation/.
2. Thomas Yellowtail, *Yellowtail, Crow Medicine Man and Sun Dance Chief: An Autobiography* (Norman: University of Oklahoma Press, 1991), 76.

Suggested Reading

The following list of books is intended to serve as a guide to discovering more deeply both the intricacies of indigenous culture and the principles and values espoused by some of our greatest thought leaders on the topic of culture and paradigm shift. There are far more books that could have been included in this list; the following are presented, however, as a short list of some of my favorites. Enjoy.

Black Elk, Wallace, and William S. Lyon. *Black Elk: The Sacred Ways of a Lakota*. New York: HarperCollins Publishers, 1991.

Brown, Tom, Jr. *The Tracker*. New York: Penguin Group, 1978.

Collins, Jim. *Good to Great*. New York: HarperCollins Publishers, 2001.

Godin, Seth. *Tribes: We Need You to Lead Us*. New York: Penguin Group, 2008.

Hshieh, Tony. *Delivering Happiness: A Path to Profits, Passion, and Purpose*. New York: Business Plus, Hachette Book Group, 2010.

Mander, Jerry. *In the Absence of the Sacred*. San Francisco: Sierra Club Books, 1991.

Peat, F. David. *Blackfoot Physics*. MA: Red Wheel/Weiser, 2005.

Pink, Daniel H. *Drive: The Surprising Truth about What Motivates Us*. New York: Penguin Group, 2009.

Quinn, Daniel. *Ishmael*. New York: Bantom/Turner, 1992.

Ruiz, Don Miguel. *The Four Agreements*. San Rafael: Amber-Allen Publishing, 1997.

Sisodia, Raj, David B. Wolfe, and Jag Sheth. *Firms of Endearment: How World-Class Companies Profit from Passion and Purpose*. Upper Saddle River, NJ: Wharton School Publishing, 2007.

About the Author

Glenn Geffcken is an accomplished executive with a background in sales, large-scale event production, publishing, and sustainability. His strengths include strategy, business development, sales coaching, finance, work-flow systems, and personnel development. Glenn spent eleven years working for a big-city newspaper during a period of great decline and upheaval in the newspaper industry. He has spent the balance of his career working mostly for entrepreneurial small firms.

In the summer of 2011, Glenn launched Balanced Is, a consulting company focusing on helping companies shift and evolve their culture, as culture leads so directly to outward results. Glenn writes a weekly blog called The Art of Balance, which is about bringing balance to business, and *SHIFT* is his first book.

In parallel to his business career, Glenn has spent many years deeply immersed in indigenous culture and spirituality, and from this has acquired a unique and insightful ability to approach businesses as living organisms in which they operate most successfully when all individual components are working in concert with the whole. Glenn calls this "holistic balance," which refers to the interdependencies of all components of a business. Glenn sees business and its role in providing livelihood, as well as necessary products and services to its customers, as a natural extension of the circle of life.

Glenn lives in the Blue Ridge Mountains of western North Carolina with his wife, Maria, and his three stepchildren, Samantha, Shana, and Kanyon. His passions are spirituality, family, ceremony, doing good in the world, sustainability, wholesome food, and motorcycles.

Open Book Editions
A Berrett-Koehler Partner

Open Book Editions is a joint venture between Berrett-Koehler Publishers and Author Solutions, the market leader in self-publishing. There are many more aspiring authors who share Berrett-Koehler's mission than we can sustainably publish. To serve these authors, Open Book Editions offers a comprehensive self-publishing opportunity.

A Shared Mission

Open Book Editions welcomes authors who share the Berrett-Koehler mission—Creating a World That Works for All. We believe that to truly create a better world, action is needed at all levels—individual, organizational, and societal. At the individual level, our publications help people align their lives with their values and with their aspirations for a better world. At the organizational level, we promote progressive leadership and management practices, socially responsible approaches to business, and humane and effective organizations. At the societal level, we publish content that advances social and economic justice, shared prosperity, sustainability, and new solutions to national and global issues.

Open Book Editions represents a new way to further the BK mission and expand our community. We look forward to helping more authors challenge conventional thinking, introduce new ideas, and foster positive change.

For more information, see the Open Book Editions website:
http://www.iuniverse.com/Packages/OpenBookEditions.aspx

Join the BK Community! See exclusive author videos, join discussion groups, find out about upcoming events, read author blogs, and much more! http://bkcommunity.com/